classic
KITCHEN
PROJECTS

classic KITCHEN PROJECTS

Complete Instructions
for 17 Distinctive Projects

NIALL BARRETT

The Taunton Press

Publisher: Jim Childs
Associate publisher: Helen Albert
Associate editor: Strother Purdy
Copy editor: Suzanne Noel
Cover and interior designer: Lori Wendin
Layout artist: Suzie Yannes
Photographer: Chris Holden
Illustrators: Niall Barrett and Bob LaPointe
Indexer: Nancy Bloomer

Taunton
BOOKS & VIDEOS
for fellow enthusiasts

Printed in the United States of America
10 9 8 7 6 5 4 3 2 1

The Taunton Press, Inc.,
63 South Main Street, PO Box 5506, Newtown, CT 06470-5506
e-mail: tp@taunton.com

Distributed by Publishers Group West

Library of Congress Cataloging-in-Publication Data

Barrett, Niall.
  Classic kitchen projects : seventeen distinctive projects from an American
craftsman / Niall Barrett.
    p. cm.
Includes index.
ISBN 1-56158-386-3
  1. Kitchen utensils. 2. Woodwork. 3. Furniture making. I. Title.
TT197.5.K57 B37 2000
643'.3—dc21   00-034335

SAFETY NOTE: Working with wood is inherently dangerous. Using hand or power tools improperly or ignoring standard safety practices can lead to permanent injury or even death. Don't try to perform operations you learn about here (or elsewhere) unless you're certain they are safe for you. If something about an operation doesn't feel right, don't do it. Look for another way. We want you to enjoy the craft, so please keep safety foremost in your mind whenever you're working with wood.

To all the little ones in my life (some of whom are not so little anymore). They give me more than they know.

ACKNOWLEDGMENTS

I WISH TO THANK my family and friends—some were gentle and some were tough, but all were supportive.

I would especially like to thank Strother Purdy for his help and encouragement above and beyond the call of duty.

Thanks to my friend and photographer Chris Holden for introducing so much clarity to this book.

I would also like to thank all the folks at The Taunton Press. Their professionalism and attention to detail made this book what it is.

Extra special credit goes to Chelsea Breeze, for brightening the world around her.

CONTENTS

INTRODUCTION

FROM THE EARLIEST open hearths to today's high-tech extravaganzas, the kitchen has always been the domestic center of any house. In fact, in colonial America, the kitchen often wasn't just the center of the house, it *was* the house: a single large room with a fireplace where people cooked, slept, and ate. Even when separate bedrooms and common rooms were added, the hub of the house remained the hearth, no doubt because it was the warmest room in winter.

The kitchen is still where family and friends are most likely to gather. Modern living rooms often lie empty while the kitchen assumes the role of social gathering place. Everything—from marriage proposals to a child's first steps—is likely to take place in the kitchen, and (oh yes) it is also where we cook and eat!

The kitchen is a socially complex place to be sure, but it's also a physically complex one. A livable/workable kitchen must be ergonomically sensible, comfortable to work in, and visually pleasing. It's not surprising, then, that we place a great deal of importance on making this space as personally efficient and visually appealing as possible.

Odds are that you are at least somewhat unsatisfied with your kitchen. Regardless of whether it is new or old, you may have found it lacking in some way. I'm not talking about anything major: Perhaps there are a few places that you can't reach comfortably, or there isn't enough counter space or not enough storage. Possibly it needs some organization or just a little dressing up.

This book begins with some ideas on planning and/or choosing the projects you might want to build and why. Advice on scale and proportion is included, in case you have to adjust the size of a project to better fit your kitchen. It also points out other ways to customize your projects (for example, by choosing different woods for different projects) and offers some thoughts on finishing options. There's also a primer on the tools, techniques, and joinery used to build the projects.

The 17 projects presented range from a simple rolling pin to a full-size kitchen island. Many of these projects can be completed in a weekend, allowing you the quick gratification that comes from successfully completing a project. Others will take longer and be more challenging, leading to even greater satisfaction. Regardless of the degree of difficulty, these projects are all attractive and useful and should be interesting and fun to build.

Additionally, these projects are designed for a space that is central to everyone's life—the kitchen—which is arguably the most social and public space in your house. And what better gallery is there for you to display your work?

PLANNING A KITCHEN

Solving Problems

DO YOU HAVE A COLLECTION OF fine wines stashed at one end of a counter, next to the empty soda bottles waiting to be returned? Would a nice wine rack give you back counter space you haven't used in ages?

Coming up with solutions to kitchen clutter starts on the drawing board.

Do your condiments, peanut-butter jars, boxes of tea, and other small kitchen necessities also congregate at one end of the counter, near the stove? Would a new shelf help you sort the clutter?

Do all your chairs have footprints on them? "Well, how else do I get to those upper shelves?" you say. You are clearly a person desperately in need of a step stool.

When you bring home groceries, do you have to leave some things in bags in a corner until you eat what you've got on your shelves to make room? More shelves are the order of the day.

Maybe you have a kitchen that works reasonably well and looks all right to boot, but the glass knobs a previous owner put on the cabinet doors in the 1950s have got to go.

Well, you get the idea. We all have kitchens that need some improvement. Once you identify the need, figuring out a solution is next. Deciding you could use a wine rack, a step stool, more shelving, or even just new cabinet knobs is the easy part. That may have been realized long ago, with daily reminders from your kitchen clutter. Creating the solution is the real issue, whether it entails finding a commercial product that fits your kitchen or figuring out something to make in your shop.

Designing a project that fits your kitchen just right is a two-part endeavor. First is the question of style: Will it go with your kitchen? Second is one of practicality: Will it

Common kitchen clutter eats up valuable counter space, making even the simplest cooking tasks a chore.

work, and will it fit into your existing space? I won't get into a long discussion on what constitutes good or bad style or the correct scale. For your kitchen, you're the best judge.

I think that most of us naturally appreciates well-designed work. If you see something that makes you quietly content, then that's it! Often nothing really jumps out at you, but in my opinion that is the essence of good design and, by definition, the correct scale and appropriate style.

It's easy to tell if something seems out of place when we see it in front of us, but it is less obvious when we don't have the finished item to look at. Try sketching the project into a close scale drawing or even onto a photograph. Or find a cardboard box or other item of similar size as the project and

Without a step stool, chairs get pressed into service to reach high shelves. Most chairs are not designed to stand on and can break under the strain.

Correct proportions are as much about looks as about practicality. This lazy Susan is obviously too large for the table, leaving no room for plates.

The same lazy Susan, on a much larger table, looks relatively small and at home.

Mocking up a counter or kitchen island helps to get the scale and location just right. You can change the setup as many times as necessary until it's just right.

place it in your room. For larger pieces, like the island or worktable in this book, try making some kind of mock-up.

When figuring out the correct size of something like a kitchen island, I will often place a piece of plywood the size of the top on some sawhorses or on a table in the space to see how well it fits. Sometimes I will go so far as to leave it in place for several days to allow people to walk around it and, if it is sturdy enough, to actually work on it.

Playing with Materials, Style, and Scale

The projects in this book cover a wide range of common organizational and cooking needs. Chances are that you'll find something just right for your kitchen and at least one or two things for which you might have a use or would build for a friend.

If you don't like a design, before you dismiss a project as unacceptable, try looking at it from another perspective. Perhaps a small

Full-size drawings are a good way to get an idea of what your finished project will look like, especially in the details. They also help in the construction because all the dimensions are right there.

change will make all the difference. Look at a similar piece that you like and ask yourself whether it is really that different or just varies in color or in size. Sometimes just changing the species of wood can alter an item's appearance. You can choose from a variety of easily available types of wood, both solid and plywood. Spending some time evaluating these can be very helpful.

Changing the size of a piece is perhaps the easiest adaptation, even though it may be one of the hardest to visualize. Strategies such as mocking up a project can be helpful in figuring out the size you need something to be, but they won't help you see how a given project will look at that size.

One of the best ways to really see how something will look is to draw it full size. This is not as crazy or as difficult as it sounds. It doesn't have to be a work of art,

just a reasonable approximation of the piece. You'll be surprised what a difference a full-size drawing can make. Details that are all but invisible on a scale drawing can suddenly have a big impact. I use large rolls of newspaper to draw on, which I get for free from a local newspaper printer before they are thrown out. But if you can't find such a source, sheets of ¼-in. lauan plywood or large, unfolded cardboard appliance boxes work just fine.

Even if something is clearly the wrong style for your kitchen, it may not take very much to make it fit. Changing the solid plywood doors on the center island to frame and panel doors, for example, would drastically change the style of the piece and would take very little extra time to do. The character of the island instantly goes from contemporary to traditional. And simply matching the wood in a project to the type of wood or color scheme you already have in your kitchen can do wonders to integrate a project.

Finishing projects for the kitchen

Sprayed finishes are the cat's pajamas for kitchens. They can be extremely durable, long lasting and look great, especially conversion varnishes and nitrocellulose lacquers. This is important because kitchen counters and cabinets get used more than any other type of furniture in the house and need to better withstand wear and tear.

Few nonprofessional woodworkers are set up to spray these types of finishes. But this is relatively easy to get around; for many years early in my woodworking career, I had no spray-finishing capacity. There are many attractive and durable oil finishes available today that are easy to apply. Even brush-on finishes are almost foolproof. Today's water-based polyurethanes, for example, produce a very attractive finish and, with a little sanding between coats, can give a good approximation of a sprayed finish.

There's another strategy of which many woodworkers may not be aware. Many professional woodworking and finishing shops are happy for a little extra business and won't charge very much to spray your completed project. Just "let your fingers do the walking" and make a few calls; you might be pleasantly surprised.

Since we are dealing with kitchen projects and, consequently, surfaces on which food is prepared, a few words about food-safe finishes are in order. There are a number of products on the market designed specifically for this purpose, which, for the most part, are fine. I use a polymerized tung oil on surfaces that will get a lot of wear, like countertops. This kind of oil finish is really tough and once cured is food-safe. For items that get cleaned frequently, like cutting boards and rolling pins, I use mineral oil. It's inexpensive, easy to renew, and also food-safe.

Brushed-on polyurethane, wiped-on oil, and sprayed lacquer are three good finish choices for kitchen projects.

Tools and Techniques

I designed the projects for this book to be relatively straightforward to make. You certainly don't need a commercial shop full of fancy tools to produce them. Almost all the joinery for the projects can be cut with a table saw, a drill press, a biscuit joiner, a router, and a hand drill. I will say that good tools yield better results and are easier to use than cheap tools, but you don't need the best of the best to get things done.

Make sure your table saw is well tuned, since much of the joinery in this book is produced using this tool. Some of the joints can be fairly exacting, so it will pay to start off with a saw cutting straight and square. Make sure the fence locks securely and is parallel to the blade; check that the blade is sharp. Also make sure you have an accurate miter gauge with an auxiliary fence. As a matter of fact, if you have ever considered upgrading your miter gauge, now is the time. Nothing will improve the quality of

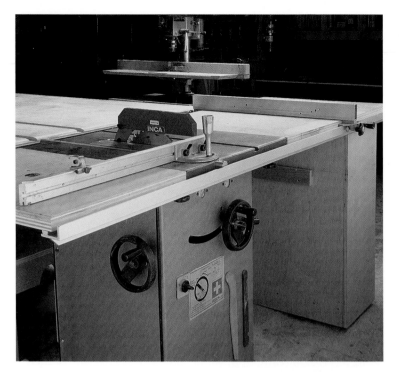

the time you spend at the table saw for as little money as a substantial and accurate miter gauge.

You will also need to build a few simple jigs. I'm not a big fan of jigs, though a lot of woodworkers love them. I know a few woodworkers who seem to do nothing but build them. Maybe that's my point: I would rather spend my time building furniture than jigs. What few jigs I do make (like the ones in this book) are usually very simple and quick to make. And I try to throw them out when the project is over so they don't multiply in the dark corners of my shop.

I also made sure to cover as many different joinery and building techniques as possible. I tried to highlight a particular type of joinery or tool technique in each project. For example, the spice drawers (see pp. 104–113) use box joints and the rolling pin (see

A cabinet saw—with a good miter gauge or other accurate crosscut setup—and drill press will be very helpful in making the projects in this book.

A plunge router, biscuit joiner, cordless drill, and lathe round out the major tooling necessary to build all of these projects.

For the projects in this book, you'll need a tapering jig, a finger-jointing jig, and a tenoning jig. All of these are easily built and extend the versatility of the table saw to shaping and cutting joinery.

pp. 12–17) is turned on a lathe. I couldn't cover every possible technique, but there is a good overview of general woodworking skills.

While sometimes challenging, the projects should not bend your brain too much. I have spent a good deal of my wood-working career building one-off pieces and working out how to do really crazy things. In a lot of ways, this book was a chance to lighten up for a while and have some fun. I trust you will enjoy yourself as much as I have!

Although the projects are all attractive and decorative, they are primarily designed to solve practical problems. So before you start building, take a moment to think about your needs. While the successful building and finishing of a project is extremely satis-fying in and of itself, it is all the more so when the end result is something you really need and get to put to good use time and time again.

FRENCH ROLLING PIN

ROLLING PINS CAN BE MADE OF almost any material, but hardwood is favored. Wooden pins season over time, and most professionals prefer their feel and maneuverability. There are many rolling-pin styles. The most familiar kind is the American or baker's rolling pin. High-quality examples of this type have sturdy handles anchored with a steel rod through the center of the pin and are fitted with ball bearings. This is the rolling pin that most of us grew up with and possibly the one you expected to see presented here.

However, many professional cooks prefer the straight French rolling pin because it allows them to get the "feel" of the dough under their palms. This is the pin you want for recalcitrant pizza dough, yeast dough, Danish pastry, puff pastry, and strudel, and it's ideal for homemade pasta. There are no handles

on this pin—the better to get a solid grip, move your hands along the barrel, put a little more pressure here, a little less there. Also, without handles, there are no unsanitary, impossible-to-clean bearings, barrel cavities, or metal axles that eventually rust.

The pin presented here is a tapered variation of the straight French pin. The classic version is about 22 in. long and tapers from 2 in. in the center to approximately 1½ in. at the ends. This design allows the pin to be rotated during the rolling process—a feature particularly useful for rolling circles of dough.

"Just a piece of wood" you say? Not so! Think of this as the BMW of rolling pins, with rack-and-pinion steering for easy maneuverability and firm-yet-supple suspension to let you feel the road—in this case, the terrain of the dough. This is the one must-have rolling pin for every cook.

FRENCH ROLLING PIN

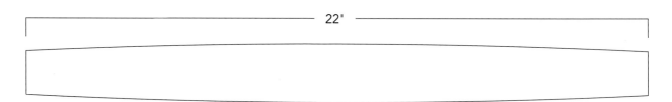

22"

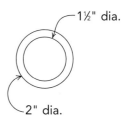

1½" dia.

2" dia.

The gently tapered shape of this rolling pin makes it superb at maneuvering around doughy terrain. It weighs about 1½ lb.

Assembling the Blank

THIS IS A VERY QUICK PROJECT to make, but first you have to decide whether to turn this pin out of a single piece of maple or to glue up a blank. I went back and forth on this decision because, although I have seen the pin made both ways, I was somewhat concerned about seasonal wood movement. In the end, I decided that, given the size of the piece, it shouldn't make much difference, as long as the grain in the glued-up version all runs in the same direction. Since I didn't have any maple large enough (8/4 isn't quite enough),

I glued up four pieces into a turning square. If you choose this approach, remember that it will probably take you longer to machine and glue up the blank for this pin than to turn it.

1. Joint and plane four pieces of maple 1⅛ in. by 1¼ in. by 22½ in.

2. Glue the pieces together in pairs so that you end up with two pieces 2¼ in. by 1¼ in. by 22½ in.

3. When these are dry, clean up the glue joints by running them through a planer until you have two pieces 2¼ in. by 1⅛ in. by 22½ in.

4. Glue these together to form a turning square 2¼ in. by 2¼ in. by 22½ in. Make sure the grain in all four pieces is correctly oriented (see "Grain Orientation").

5. When the turning square is dry, scrape off the glue and square up the ends, making sure to leave at least ¼ in. extra in length. This extra will be removed at the end along with the turning-center marks that remain on the ends.

CUT LIST FOR FRENCH ROLLING PIN		
4 Turning blank parts	22" x 1⅛" x 1¼"	solid maple
Other materials		
Vegetable oil or mineral oil		

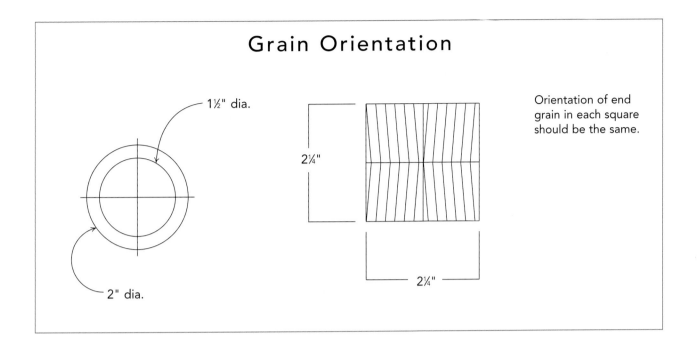

Grain Orientation

1½" dia.

2" dia.

2¼"

2¼"

Orientation of end grain in each square should be the same.

Turning the Pin

1. Mount the glued-up blank on the lathe.

2. Using a roughing-out gouge, turn it into a cylinder. At this point, it should still be a little more than 2 in. in diameter.

3. Using a pencil, mark the blank in the center then measure out 11 in. to the left and right. This defines the length of your pin.

4. Place a mark at $3^{11}/_{16}$ in. and $7^{5}/_{16}$ in. from each end mark. If you have four pairs of calipers, set one to each of the following dimensions: 2 in., 1⅞ in., 1¾ in., and 1½ in. If you have only one pair of calipers, you will have to reset it for each of these measurements as you work.

5. Starting with the center mark, cut a groove using a parting tool (most parting tools are ³⁄₁₆ in. to ¼ in. wide) until the diameter at the bottom of the groove is 2 in. Use the 2-in. calipers to check this often.

6. When the pair of calipers just slips over the piece with a touch of friction, it's done.

7. One by one, moving out from this center groove, make grooves at your marks of

PHOTO A: Use a parting tool to cut the different-diameter grooves that shape the pin. (Note that the pin shown is a slightly longer version of the pin described in the instructions.)

Turning Sequence

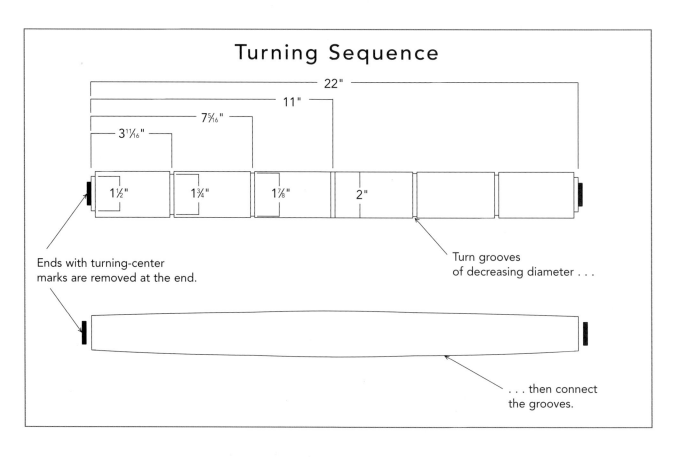

22"

11"

7⁵⁄₁₆"

3¹¹⁄₁₆"

1½"   1¾"   1⅞"   2"

Ends with turning-center
marks are removed at the end.

Turn grooves
of decreasing diameter . . .

. . . then connect
the grooves.

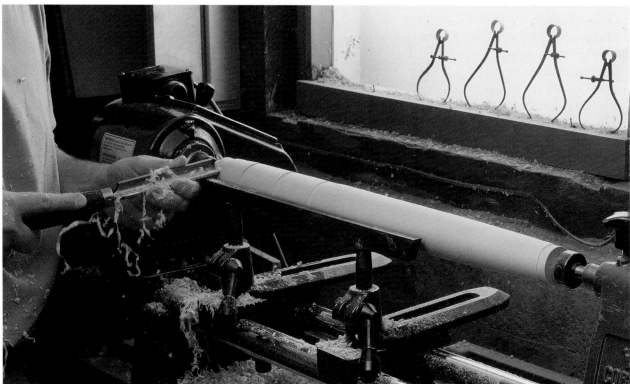

PHOTO B: Use a gouge to shape the gentle taper by cutting until you reach the depth of the grooves.

decreasing diameter using the appropriate caliper setting (see **photo A** on p. 15 and "Turning Sequence").

8. Make a step at each end to better define the finished length. The diameter of this step is not critical as long as it is large enough to hold the lathe centers.

9. Working your way out from the center of the pin, use the roughing-out gouge to connect the grooves in a flowing taper. Let the cut get slightly deeper toward the ends, and blend the grooves together until you have a rough approximation of the shape of the pin (see **photo B**).

10. Switch to a skew or a scraper, whichever you are more comfortable with, and finish shaping the curve. You are not necessarily looking for absolute perfection, but the closer you can get to a smooth, even curve that is the same on both sides, the better your pin will work and look. You should be able to see any large difference, but the minor undulations in the shape are easier to find by running your hand over the piece. (Not while it's spinning, please!)

11. When you are happy with the shape, sand the piece from 80 grit through at least 150 grit before you remove it from the lathe. The smoother the finish is, the better working pin you will have.

12. Remove the pin from the lathe, and cut off the extra length with a handsaw.

13. Sand the ends smooth, and apply the finish.

Finishing and Seasoning the Pin

Your new rolling pin should be seasoned with a light coat of vegetable oil. Thereafter, it will darken to a lovely amber color as it ages. I would not normally suggest this type of oil because, if left for too long, vegetable

STRAIGHT PIN OPTION

For those of you that might want to turn a straight pin instead of a tapered version, it's a simple matter of omitting the tapering steps. I must confess, though, that I find it much more difficult to turn a near-perfect cylinder than a tapered shape. Tapers hide minor variations much better than perfect cylinders.

oil will turn rancid. This is unpleasant at best. Assuming that you will use and clean your pin often, this will not be an issue. If you don't use a rolling pin that often, then I suggest you use mineral oil.

As kitchen gear goes, the French pin is low maintenance, but as with any rolling pin it will need some attention after each use, particularly if you use it with a soft, stick-to-the-pin type of dough. Resist the urge to scrub the pin with lots of soapy water. Not only is it unwise to soak the wood, but wet pastry bits are harder to remove than dry ones.

It's okay to use a damp cloth on the pin, and it's fine to scrape off the stuck-on stuff with a dough scraper or the straight side of a kitchen knife. While scraping, however, take care not to nick or (worse) gouge the wood. A smooth, clean surface is vital for a fine rolling pin.

Also, ignore any instruction in a recipe that directs you to use a rolling pin to crush peppercorns, spices, or nuts. A rolling pin is not the best tool for this job, and you will damage the surface of your pin.

CUTTING BOARD AND KNIFE RACK

THESE TWO PROJECTS GO hand-in-hand. After all, to cut and chop food you need both knives and a cutting board. Nevertheless, they are independent projects and may be built separately.

If you buy a "butcher block" cutting board these days, chances are what you'll get is a board with lengthwise strips of wood glued together. If you have ever seen a real butcher block, as in the one really used by butchers, you may have noticed that it is rather different. A true butcher block is constructed of many pieces of wood arranged so that the grain of the wood runs vertically (up and down).

End grain is a superior cutting surface because it is able to "heal" itself. When the knife strikes this type of surface during cutting, the grain of the wood actually separates and then closes when the knife is removed. The wood itself is not cut; instead, you are cutting between the fibers. This ensures that knives keep their edge and that knife scars heal to maintain a clean working surface.

In contrast, "butcher blocks" made with the grain running lengthwise don't last. When drawing a knife across this surface, the wood fibers are cut slightly, creating a permanent wound. Over time, with thousands of cuts on the surface, the block will scar substantially, giving food places to lodge, and will deteriorate rather badly over the years.

Having said all this, it is quite a bit more work to produce a true butcher block. However, I thought it would be worth doing on a smaller scale. The construction process is interesting, and the surface created is extremely attractive. Think of this cutting board as a butcher block for your counter.

CUTTING BOARD

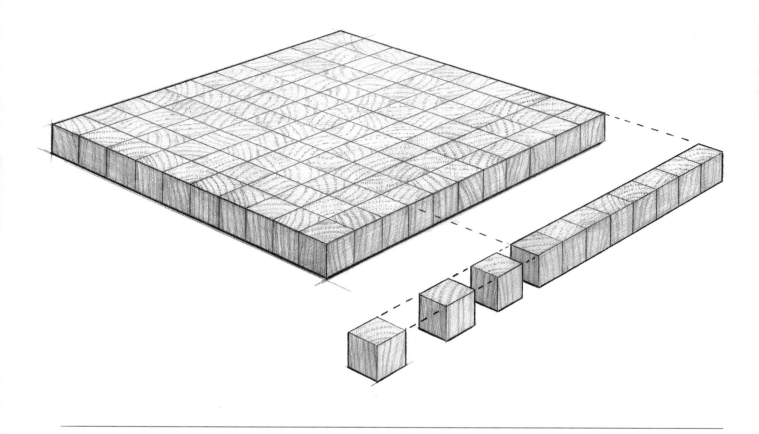

Making the Plank

THE FIRST STEP IN MAKING this cutting board is to build a conventional plank with edge-grain construction. Make sure that the strips are straight, flat, and square so that the glued-up top will be also. You might be tempted to use biscuits or dowels to align the pieces, but

don't. You will be recutting this top and reassembling it; any biscuits or dowels would show.

1. Rip 8/4 flatsawn stock into 11 strips, approximately 2 in. wide and 24 in. long.

2. Joint and thickness-plane the strips to 1¹³⁄₁₆ in. by 1¹³⁄₁₆ in.

3. Glue them together to produce a quartersawn top 20 in. wide, 1¹³⁄₁₆ in. thick, and 24 in. long. (By "quartersawn," I mean that all the end grain should run perpendicular to the face of the assembled butcher block.) You will have less trouble if you glue up these pieces a couple at a time until you have the top completed.

4. When the top is complete and the glue is dry, clean the top and flatten any minor irregularities with a belt sander or (preferably) a handplane. Be very careful with all

Top and Side Views

The handsome end-grain cutting surface of this board
doesn't show knife marks and will last a lifetime.

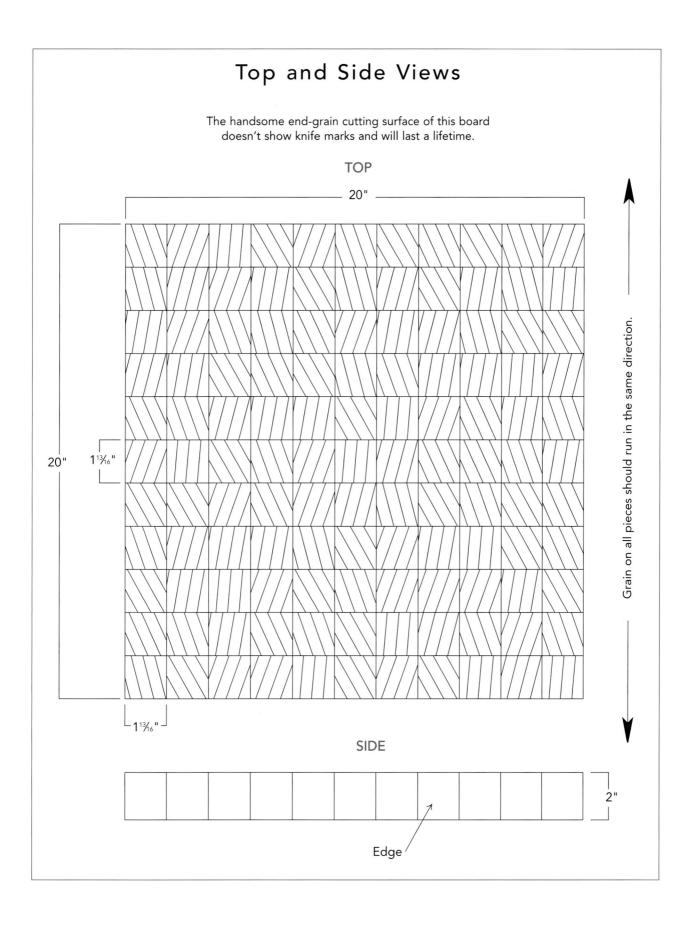

TOP

20"

20"

1¹³⁄₁₆"

1¹³⁄₁₆"

Grain on all pieces should run in the same direction.

SIDE

2"

Edge

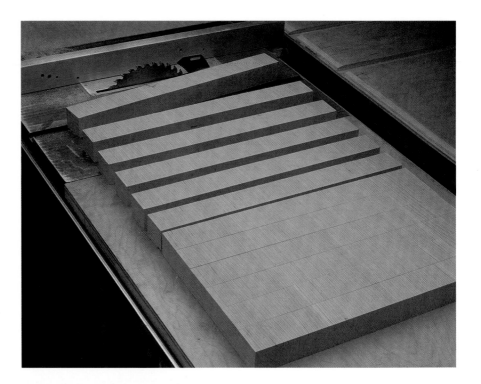

PHOTO A: Crosscut the glued-up blank into 2-in.-wide strips.

PHOTO B: Turn the strips on edge, and arrange them until the grain patterns are pleasing.

this; it's crucial that the top and bottom surfaces be flat and parallel for the next step. If you have access to a wide belt sander or a planer wide enough to handle this piece, then by all means take advantage of it.

5. Square up one end of this perfect plank.

6. Crosscut the plank into 2-in.-wide pieces (see **photo A**).

7. Take these pieces and turn them so that their end grain is facing up.

8. Rearrange them to form a 20-in. by 20-in. by 2-in. square. I think it looks better if the end-grain squares look randomly placed, so move the parts around until you get a pleasing arrangement. When you are satisfied with how your block looks, glue the parts together, as in step 3 (see **photo B**).

Flattening the Top

Once your cutting board is assembled and the glue is dry, it's time to flatten and smooth the top and bottom surfaces. The hardest way to do this is also the most satisfying, since it leaves an absolutely exquisite surface. I'm talking, of course, about hand-

POLYURETHANE GLUE

Polyurethane glue is useful to glue up butcher-block tops for a number of reasons:

• Polyurethane is waterproof. Cutting boards will probably be cleaned and wiped down often with water.

• It's a single-part glue. There are other waterproof glues available, but most require mixing two parts. With polyurethane glue, there's no mixing involved.

• It has a reasonable open time. When you're rushing to put clamps on before the glue sets, you'll appreciate this feature.

• It's easy to spread; in fact, it acts as something of a lubricant in bringing joints together. It doesn't grab like a polyvinyl acetate (PVA) glue, so you can easily and more accurately line up and position the parts.

• You only have to spread polyurethane on one of the mating surfaces (something you will appreciate when gluing up this top!).

• As it cures, the glue expands into the wood fibers, strengthening the bond.

• It needs only minimum clamping pressure, requiring only that the parts be firmly held together. In fact, if you use too much clamping pressure, you'll starve the joint and get a poor bond.

• Dried polyurethane is extremely easy to work; it won't clog your sandpaper or dull your cutting tools.

• On the down side, it doesn't clean up with water. Keep a rag and a can of acetone handy to wipe away glue squeeze-out and, if necessary, to clean your hands and clothes.

To ensure a good bond with polyurethane glue, remember that it cures in the presence of moisture. If the wood and/or the environment is particularly dry, try spraying a small amount of water onto the mating portion of the joint before clamping.

Polyurethane glues also like a little "tooth" or roughness to the joint. As the glue expands, it gets into and around this tooth and forms a mechanical bond. If your wood is glass smooth, the glue can't penetrate well and you could get a joint failure. For a piece that has been through the planer, a light scuffing of the surface with a piece of 80-grit sandpaper will give you enough tooth. Parts directly off the table saw are perfect just as they are.

planing! It takes a sharp plane, some time, and a lot of elbow grease, but nothing else will produce as nice a finish. A handplaned finish on side grain is a sweet thing, but a well-executed, handplaned finish on end grain leaves the cherry feeling and looking like polished stone. It is quite astounding!

1. Set a smooth plane to take very thin shavings. I use a Record #4½ (Stanley makes an almost identical version). This is a slightly larger version of the #4 smooth plane. It is 10½ in. long and 2⅜ in. wide. The extra weight and size coupled with a wider-than-normal blade make it a good choice for this type of work, where you have a large, difficult surface to plane. The extra blade width makes it a little harder to push, but in this case you will be taking very light shavings. Regardless of your plane choice, it has to be extremely sharp and well tuned; you will probably have to hone it a couple of times during the work.

2. Always work toward the center of the piece to avoid breaking out the edges. Then just work the piece bit by bit until it is smooth and beautiful (see **photo C**).

Just so you don't think that I'm a hand-plane nut, I'll tell you how to get a really nice finish with less work: Just sand it (though, it's still not as easy as it sounds!).

1. With a belt sander, flatten the surface with 80 grit sandpaper.
2. Then work your way up to 120 grit with the belt sander.
3. Switch to a finish sander, preferably a random orbit.
4. Go back to 100 grit and get rid of all the belt-sander marks. Then work your way up to 320 grit (or 400 grit, if you can stand it), at which point you will have a good approximation of the planed finish.

For those of you that think that this is all crazy—seeing that this is a cutting board after all and will be chopped and hacked daily—I have a third option for you: Just stop sanding when the board is flat and reasonably smooth.

Finishing

I finished this cutting board with some mineral oil, which is food-safe and attractive. There are a number of other food-safe finishes on the market, but mineral oil is inexpensive and easily available. This is important since you will have to reoil your block fairly often if you use it a lot.

PHOTO C: The time and effort necessary to handplane end grain pay off with a glass-smooth finish.

MAINTAINING A WOOD TOP IN THE KITCHEN

Hardwood cutting surfaces are very attractive and durable, but are wooden surfaces sanitary or difficult to maintain? Although there is some controversy as to whether wooden cutting boards are sanitary compared to plastic ones, wood ones are safe enough if taken care of properly.

Simple use of normal hygiene (soap and water) when cleaning any cutting surface is certainly in order. I also periodically use a weak solution of bleach (10 parts water to 1 part bleach). The solution won't harm the wood, and it helps keep the bacteria under control.

If your cutting board appears a bit dull after repeated use and cleaning, a simple reapplication of mineral oil (which is sanitary and food-safe) will brighten the finish and nourish the surface.

One last point: If and when your board gets to the point where you feel it is too unsightly, you can just turn it over and use the other surface. When that side needs to be spruced up, simply resurface it. Since it's 2 in. thick, you will be able to do this many times.

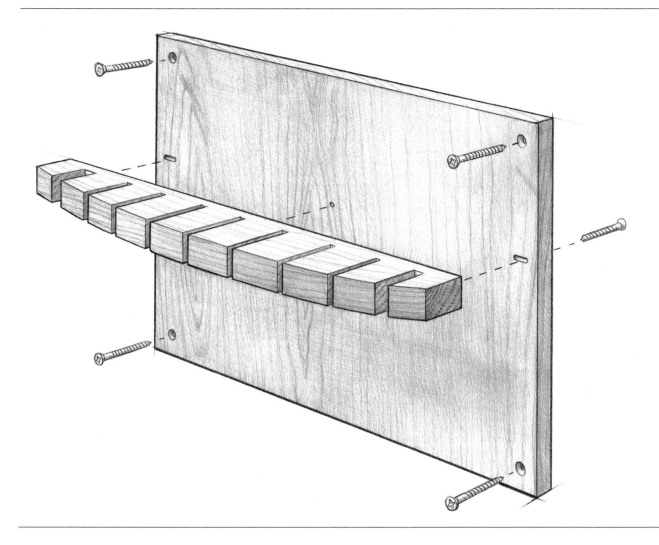

Construction and Assembly

I HAVE ALWAYS LIKED THE NOTION of a knife rack: a special place to keep kitchen knives safe, sharp, and accessible. Good knives are expensive, and the idea of just throwing them into a drawer seems disrespectful at best.

The problem is that most knife racks or holders either take up counter space (as in your common knife block) or hide the blades of the knives (clearly a safety measure), forcing you to identify a knife by its

CUT LIST FOR KNIFE RACK			
1	Back	¾" x 18" x 20"	solid cherry
1	Knife holder	19¾" x 1½" x 3½"	solid cherry
Other materials			
	Polymerized tung oil		
2	Wood screws		#8 x 2"
1	Wood screw		#8 x 1"
4	Brass panhead screws with washers		#8 x 2"

Top, Elevation, and Side Views

This rack keeps knives safe but within reach. The blades are visible to help you pick out the right knife. It can accommodate knives of any size, plus two sharpening steels.

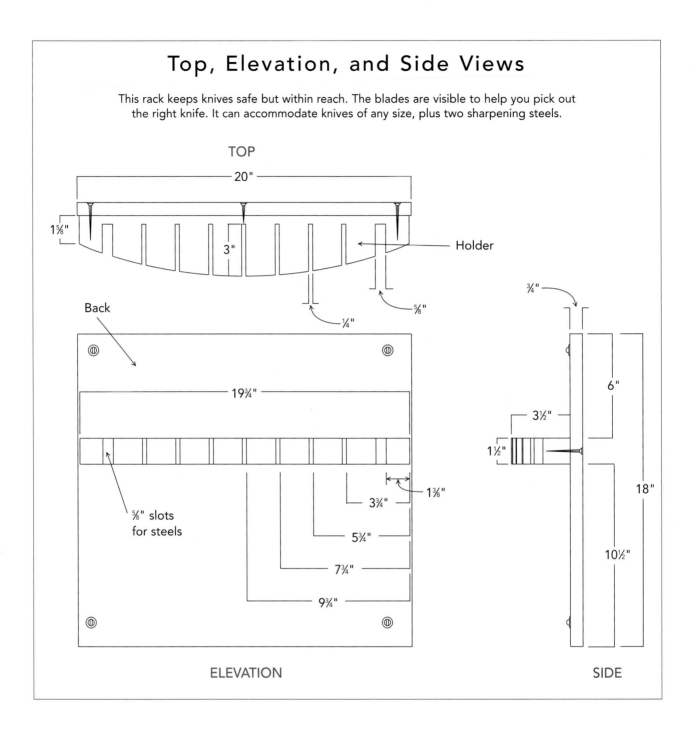

TOP

20"

1⅝"

3"

Holder

¼"

⅝"

Back

¾"

19¾"

6"

3½"

1½"

⅝" slots
for steels

1⅞"

3¾"

18"

5¾"

7¾"

10½"

9¾"

ELEVATION

SIDE

handle. To overcome these issues, I designed a rack that mounts on the backsplash under the cabinets at the back of the counter. This location reduces clutter on the counter and keeps knives within arm's reach but out of the reach of small children; with the blades visible, it is easy to identify the knife you wish to use.

Knife Holder

1. Joint and plane a piece of cherry to 3½ in. by 1½ in. by 19¾ in.

2. Place a ¼-in. dado blade in your table saw, set to a height of 3 in.

3. Set your table-saw fence to the largest of the slot-position dimensions. This will be the center slot.

PHOTO D: Cut the slots for the knife blades on the table saw while the workpiece is still square.

4. Place the workpiece against your miter gauge, set at 90 degrees, with the end against the fence, and make the first slot cut. Make sure you place a piece of scrap wood behind the workpiece to avoid tearout when the sawblade exits the workpiece.

5. Reposition the fence to the next smallest dimension, and make the next cut.

6. Without changing the position of the fence, rotate the workpiece so that the opposite end is against the fence, and make a cut.

7. Repeat this sequence until you get to the smallest dimension. The procedure is the same for these cuts, but you will need to change to a ⅝-in. dado blade. The ⅝-in. slots are designed to hold sharpening steels but will hold other items as well, such as a carving fork (see **photo D**).

8. Lay out the curve on the front of the piece that goes from the center of the front of the piece to 1⅝ in. from the back at each end.

9. Carefully cut about 1/16 in. from the line using a bandsaw (see **photo E**). A jigsaw or a coping saw will also work.

10. Sand to the line, and continue to finish-sand the entire piece to 150 grit.

PHOTO E: Guide the workpiece smoothly through the band-saw to ensure an even curve on the front edge.

DESIGN OPTIONS: SMALLER HOLDER AND ALTERNATE HOLDER

Smaller Holder

It occurred to me while building the knife holder that by simply making the back of this holder smaller you can put it other places in the kitchen. You could still place it where I have suggested, but with a smaller back you could move it to another wall-mounted location without it looking out of place, as it would with the full back. The full back does provide some extra wall protection, but otherwise it should work the same (see photo).

Alternate Holder

I spent a great deal of time determining the best layout of slots to hold the most different kinds and sizes of knives. While I settled on the one presented in this chapter, it was by no means the only configuration I came up with. One other slot configuration I particularly liked is shown here (see "Optional Knife Holder").

I ended up not using this holder because it requires the knives be lifted clear rather than just pulled forward from the slots. This would

not have worked for the location I chose, but would be a good choice for a closed box holder or a straight counter insert. You would have to make a template for routing the slots. Alternatively you could drill a hole at the ends of the slots, carefully cut them out with a jigsaw, then file and sand to the lines. This holder accommodates nine knives, one cleaver, and two sharpening steels.

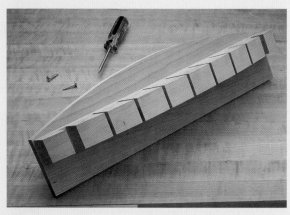

A shorter back works as well as a full back and offers a different look, though it provides less wall protection.

Optional Knife Holder

TOP VIEW

12"

2⅝"

This holder is 1¼" thick and can accommodate five slots 3" x ¼", two slots 1½" x ¼", two slots 1" x ¼", one slot 4½" x ⁵⁄₁₆", and two holes for sharpening steels ⅝" dia.

Back

The back is nothing more than a piece of cherry 20 in. wide by 18 in. long by ¾ in. thick. You can adjust the length to suit the space you have available, but make sure you have enough height for the longest knife you wish to store. I placed the top of the holder 6 in. down from the top of the back, which works for my knives. You may have to adjust this slightly up or down.

The knife holder is attached to the back with three screws, through the back and into the holder. You may have noticed that the holder is ¼ in. shorter than the back is wide. This is to allow the back to move seasonally and not have the holder stick out past the edge of the back, if the back shrinks.

1. Joint, plane, and edge-glue enough cherry stock to produce a blank big enough for the back.

2. Trim the blank to size, and finish-sand it.

3. Drill and countersink a hole for a center screw. Use a shorter screw, so as not to invade the center slot.

4. In order for the back to be able to move freely with seasonal wood movement, horizontally elongate the two outer attachment screw holes. Drill and countersink two overlapping holes for the screws on the ends (see **photo F**).

Finishing

I finished this piece with a polymerized tung oil, but any quality furniture oil will do. You don't need a food-safe oil, since you will not be preparing food on your knife rack. You do, however, want an oil that will wear well. You don't want to have to take this rack down too often to re-oil it.

Attach the rack to the wall using four decorative, brass panhead screws with washers, one in each corner. Be sure to elongate the screw holes before to allow for movement. The washers will cover the holes.

PHOTO F: Cut elongated screw slots at the ends of the back to allow for seasonal wood movement.

ADJUSTABLE SHELVES

HAD BEEN TRYING TO WORK out a really simple (read "fast") way to make an elegant wooden version of the old standby, metal standards and brackets. Although I have seen many commercial versions of wall-hung shelving systems built of wood, I wanted something cleverly uncomplicated (if you know what I mean). The problem was always the shelf support brackets. What I needed was a way to hold up the shelves that didn't rely on brackets.

Luckily, I got this flash of insight. Why not just make couple of uprights with matching notches in them and stick the shelves into the notches? As long as the shelves fit the notches just right and weren't too deep or heavily loaded, it should be fine.

The physics of it seem to work: The notches support the shelves and hold quite a lot of weight. The first time I made it, however, installing it on the wall proved somewhat difficult. Once you cut notches in the uprights, they become more flexible. When you screw these flexible pieces of wood to a not-so-flat wall, the notches either spread open or pinch closed just enough to make the shelves either too loose or too tight in their slots. And, when open, the shelves slide easily from side to side.

In keeping with the original spirit of this project, the solution to these issues turned out to be simple. A spline inserted into the back of each upright stiffens them so they do not bend, and matching notches in the backs of the shelves keep them from moving side to side. The arrangement also has the added benefit of being rigid enough that the whole unit can be hung from just two points at the tops of the uprights. So, with several refinements, I present you with amazingly simple adjustable shelves!

ADJUSTABLE SHELVES

The shelves fit into notches in the uprights and are cantilevered.
There are no brackets or other hardware to hold the shelves in place.

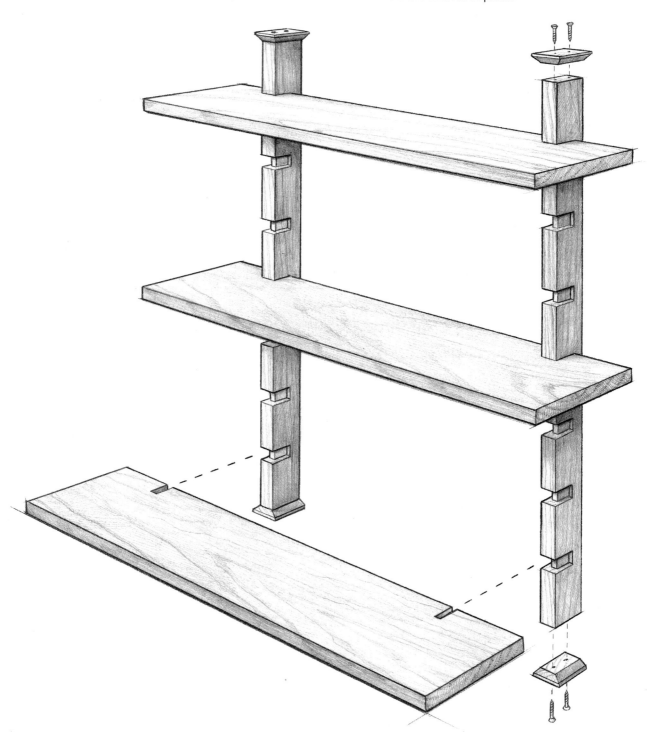

Front and Side Views

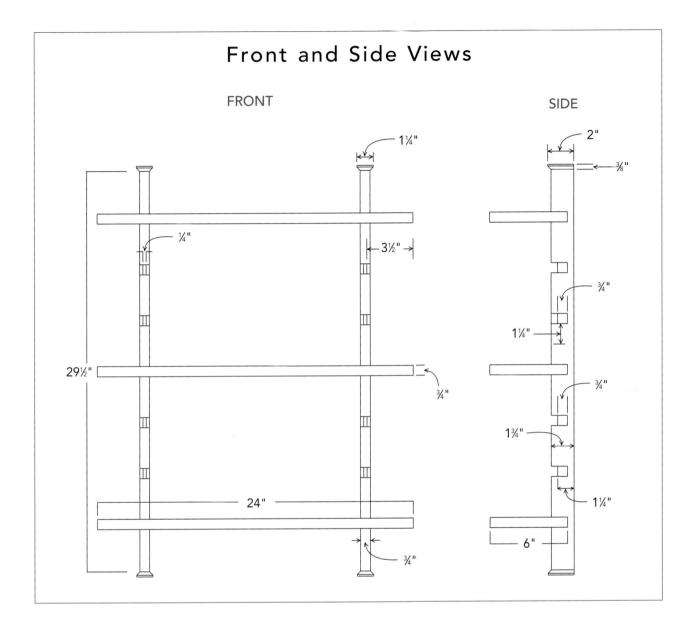

FRONT

SIDE

Stock Preparation

ALL THE PARTS SHOULD BE first milled to size, and then shaped accordingly. I find it's more efficient to do the bulk of the jointing, planing, ripping, and crosscutting work at the same time.

1. Mill the uprights to their finished size.

2. Cut the shelves to width and length, but leave them a little thicker than ¾ in. for now.

3. Mill the spline material, again leaving each piece a little thick, wide, and long.

CUT LIST FOR ADJUSTABLE SHELVES			
2	Uprights	1¾" x 29½" x ¾"	solid oak
3	Shelves	6" x 24" x ¾"	solid oak
4	Caps	1¼" x 2" x ⅜"	solid oak
2	Splines	1¼" x 29½" x ¼"	solid oak
Other materials			
2	Keyhole hangers and screws		
8	#8 x ¾" brass screws (to attach caps)		

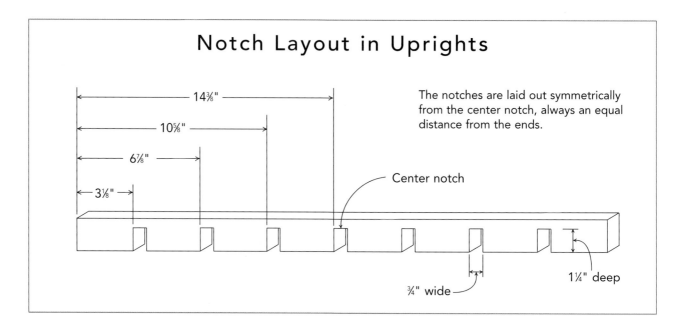

Notch Layout in Uprights

14⅜"

10⅝"

6⅞"

3⅛"

The notches are laid out symmetrically from the center notch, always an equal distance from the ends.

Center notch

¾" wide

1¼" deep

PHOTO A: Cut the shelf notches in the uprights with a dado blade on the table saw.

1. Clamp the uprights together to cut notches in them simultaneously. This will ensure that the joints line up with each other and the shelves are parallel.

2. Cut the notches an equal distance from either end of the uprights. This makes it possible to cut a notch in each end of the uprights for each setup. I used a flip stop on my miter gauge to register each series of cuts, but you can also use the table-saw fence for registration (see **photo A**).

3. Cut the last notch in the center of the uprights.

Splines

1. Install a ¼-in.-wide dado blade in your table saw; set it to the same 1¼-in. height as in the previous setup.

2. Position the fence to make a cut down the center of the back edge of the uprights.

3. Cut the groove for the splines in each upright.

4. Plane the spline material until it's easily pressed by hand into this groove. Don't make the spline too thick because the glue will swell it slightly and it will grab as you insert the spline.

4. Make one long piece 1¼ in. wide and ⅜ in. thick for the caps. Make enough stock to cut four caps plus a couple of extras.

The Uprights

To cut ¾-in.-wide by 1¼-in.-deep notches for the shelves in the uprights, use a dado blade on your table saw and a miter gauge (see "Notch Layout in Uprights").

PHOTO B: Gently tap overlong splines into the uprights. Clamp the uprights across their faces so they don't bulge while the glue sets.

5. Insert the dry splines about halfway into the grooves.

6. Spread glue on both sides of the part of each spline that remains exposed. It is important to apply the glue in this manner. The splines do not need much to keep them in place; if you put too much glue into these joints it will only end up squeezing out in the dadoes and around the visible portions of the splines, which will be extremely difficult to clean up!

7. Tap the spline in the rest of the way until it bottoms out in the cut (see **photo B**). You may have to put it in a vise or use some clamps to get it in all the way.

8. Once the splines are fully seated, place some clamps along the joint to make sure it remains tight until the glue dries.

9. Once the glue is dry, trim the excess off the splines. A sharp handsaw for the ends and a block plane for the back will make short work of this.

Shelves

1. Shim the ¼-in. dado blade so it will make a cut just a little wider than the slot the spline fits into. This will allow the notches you will cut in the shelves to fit easily over the splines.

2. Lower the blade to cut ¾ in. deep, and set the table-saw fence 3½ in. from the blade.

3. Using a miter gauge with a tall auxiliary face attached to support the shelves, cut a notch in each end of the back of all the shelves (see **photo C** on p. 36).

4. Take these still slightly thick shelves and plane them down until they fit easily into the notches of the uprights. They should slide in easily but not be too loose.

Remember that these shelves still need to be sanded and that it doesn't take much for these shelves to be too loose (see "Shelf Connection Detail" on p. 36).

PHOTO C: With a ¼-in. dado blade, notch the backs of shelves to fit over the splines. Use the rip fence to ensure the notches are an equal distance from the ends of all the shelves.

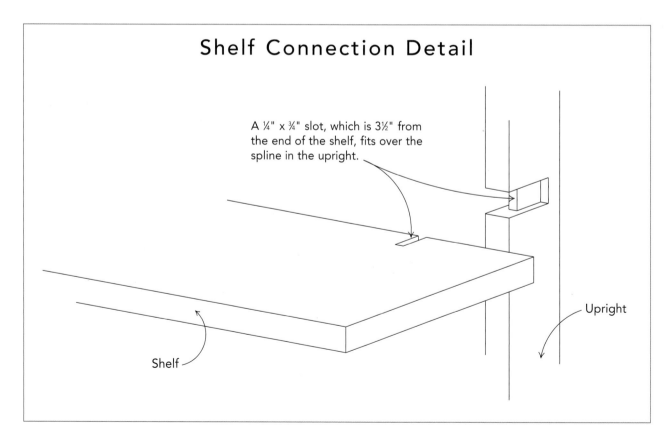

Shelf Connection Detail

A ¼" x ¾" slot, which is 3½" from the end of the shelf, fits over the spline in the upright.

Upright

Shelf

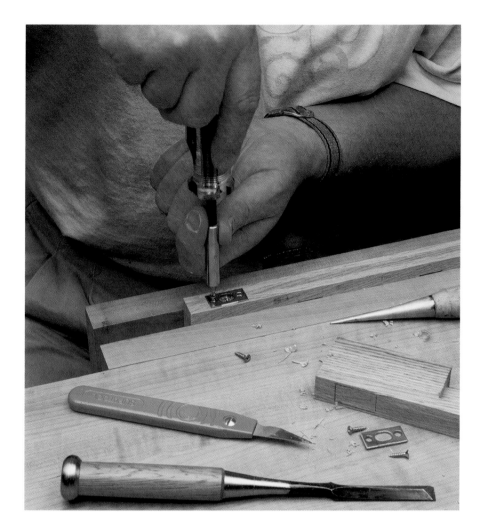

PHOTO D: Install hanger hardware flush with the back side of the uprights.

Hangers

The next step is to install some metal hangers in the top back of each upright. There are several types of hangers available from woodworking suppliers, and the exact installation method will depend on the type you choose. You will need to choose a flush hanger, however, to allow the shelves to hang flat against the wall. A typical installation requires you to mortise the hanger into the workpiece.

1. With a sharp marking knife, trace the outline of the hanger onto the top back of each upright.

2. Using a sharp chisel, remove enough material to allow the hangers to be installed flush.

3. Drill a hole inside each mortise deep and large enough to allow each hanger to fit over a screw head.

4. Screw the hangers in place (see **photo D**).

Decorative Caps

1. Bevel both long edges of the cap stock on your table saw with the blade tilted 45 degrees. This bevel should leave the narrow side of the stock $^{13}/_{16}$ in. wide (just slightly wider than the uprights). It should also leave a right angle flat along each long edge $^{1}/_{8}$ in. wide.

2. With the blade still tilted, transfer the workpiece to your miter gauge set at 90 degrees, and cut a matching bevel on each end (see "Making the Caps" on p. 38).

Making the Caps

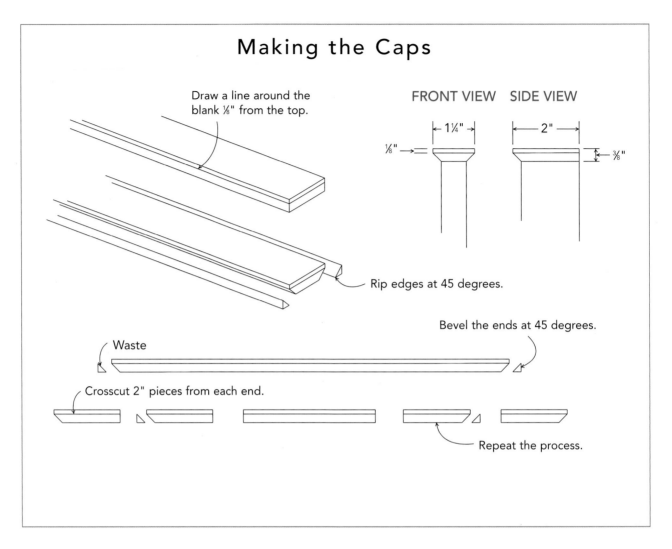

Draw a line around the blank ⅛" from the top.

FRONT VIEW SIDE VIEW

1¼"

2"

⅛"

⅜"

Rip edges at 45 degrees.

Bevel the ends at 45 degrees.

Waste

Crosscut 2" pieces from each end.

Repeat the process.

PHOTO E: Install the top and bottom end caps with two brass screws.

DESIGN OPTION: LARGE OR SMALL?

The shelves in this chapter are relatively small, but I have built several different sizes of this kind of shelving, including some quite large (see the photo).

You can certainly make a unit as tall as your ceiling height will allow, but shelves deeper than 9 in. should be avoided. You could possibly make them a little deeper, by making the uprights larger and deeper (the ones in the photo are 2½ in. deep and 1½ in. wide), but I think the scale would look wrong.

A shelf length of 48 in. is the maximum for a unit with two uprights—as long as you keep 30 in. between upright centers and 9 in. on each side. If you want a wider unit, you will have to use more uprights. All of this is assuming ¾-in.-thick shelves. You can use thicker shelves, but you really gain very little since the thicker shelves are heavier. I also think the lighter look of ¾-in. shelves is more in keeping with the simple, open spirit of the piece.

A much larger version of the adjustable-shelf project, used to hold this antique-radio collection. It isn't a good idea to make this type of shelf much larger than this.

---

3. Crosscut a 2-in. piece off of each end, and repeat the process until you have enough caps for the project and a couple of extras. I recommend cutting extra because it only takes a few moments to do, and these little pieces can sometimes split when you drill holes for the attachment screws.

4. Drill two countersunk holes for some small brass screws and some mating pilot holes into the ends of the uprights, and attach the caps (see **photo E**).

Sanding and Finishing

Sand all the parts to at least 150 grit. You might find it easier to temporarily remove the caps for sanding and even finishing, and you should definitely remove the hangers for finishing. I finished my shelves with a satin spray lacquer, but as with many of the projects in this book, a good-quality oil finish or even a carefully applied brush-on water-based polyurethane would also work well.

WINE RACK

WINE CELLARS ARE ROMANTIC places. Dusty bottles sleep in orderly rows in a dark, moist, cool climate, waiting to be dusted off, brought upstairs, and enjoyed.

But you don't really need a fancy, expensive cellar to store and age your wines. In fact, not all wines are meant to be aged. If you're like most wine consumers, you'll enjoy your wines soon after you bring them home. A relatively small wine rack, located in an appropriate place, will be fine for housing your wines.

Wine cellars are ideal places to store wine. But it's possible to store wine upstairs quite well by keeping a few things in mind. Temperature fluctuations, sunlight, and movement are the biggest enemies of wine.

People commonly make the mistake of storing wine in a rack in a brightly lit room where it gets both hot and cold. It may look nice, but the wine will turn quickly. Ultraviolet light will penetrate even dark-colored glass, so avoid direct sunlight.

Ideal storage temperature is between 55°F and 65°F. More importantly, the temperature should be constant. A slow change of 10 or so degrees between seasons is not a big problem. But this kind of fluctuation on a regular basis will damage your wines.

Lastly, vibration disturbs a red wine's sediment and can be harmful to all wines, so the top of your refrigerator is not the best location.

This rack will hold about 17 bottles of wine and, like all good wine-rack designs, stores the wine horizontally so that the wine stays in contact with the cork. This prevents the cork from drying and shrinking, which would allow air to enter the bottle and negatively affect the wine's flavor. The solid sides keep the wine in relative shade.

WINE RACK

This mahogany wine rack will store
at least 17 bottles of wine horizontally.
The solid sides keep most light out.

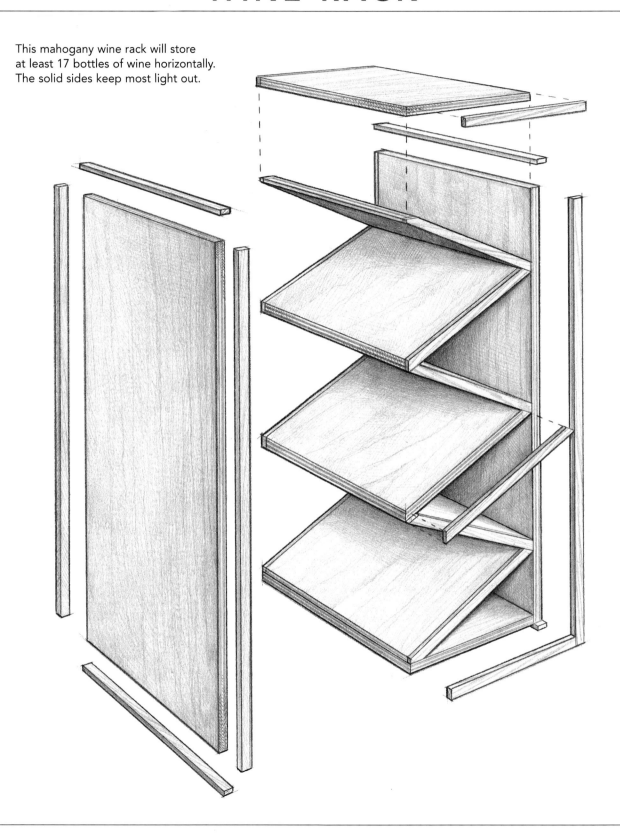

Front and Side Views

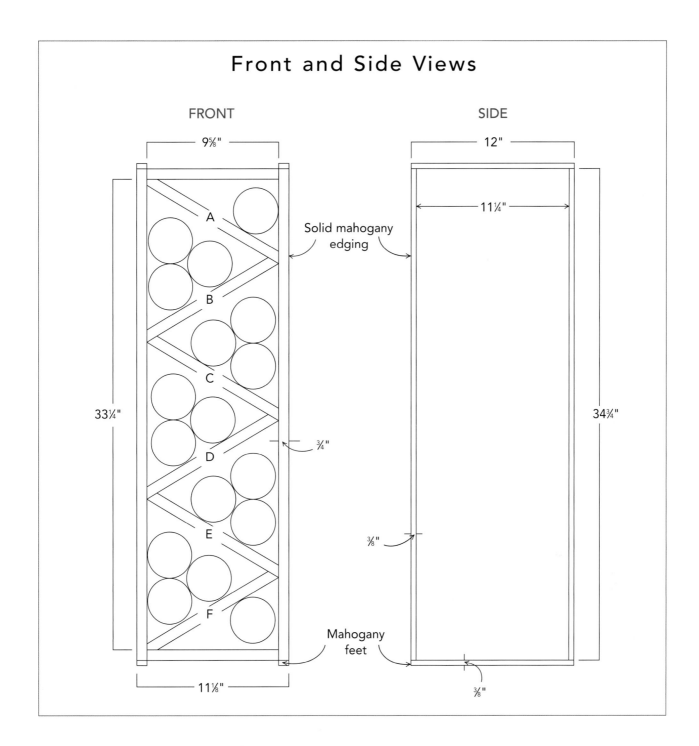

FRONT

SIDE

9⅝"

12"

11¼"

Solid mahogany edging

A

B

C

D

E

F

33¼"

34¾"

¾"

⅜"

11⅛"

Mahogany feet

⅜"

Construction and Assembly

WHILE THIS DESIGN LOOKS simple, it's a little tricky to build. If you follow my directions precisely, though, I guarantee it will all work out. It's a matter of accuracy: The interior dimensions of the box have to be exactly as given in the drawing. The space thus created is precisely the right size to hold the partitions, provided they are cut to the right size and their angles are exact (see "Exact Partition Sizes" on p. 44). If the box size changes slightly, the length of and angles on the ends of the partitions must also slightly

CUT LIST FOR WINE RACK			
2	Top and bottom	9⅝" x 11¼"x ¾"	mahogany plywood
2	Sides	34¾" x 11¼" x ¾"	mahogany plywood
5	Partitions	11⅛" x 10½" x ¾"	mahogany plywood
1	Top partition	11⅛" x 10½" x ¾"	mahogany plywood
4	Feet	12" x ⅜" x 13⁄16"	solid mahogany
20 linear ft.	Edging	⅜" x ¾"	solid mahogany
Other materials			
12	Brass screws	#10 x ¾"	

Exact Partition Sizes

All partitions are cut on the ends at 60 degrees. The last cuts on partitions A and F are at 90 degrees to the 60-degree cut.

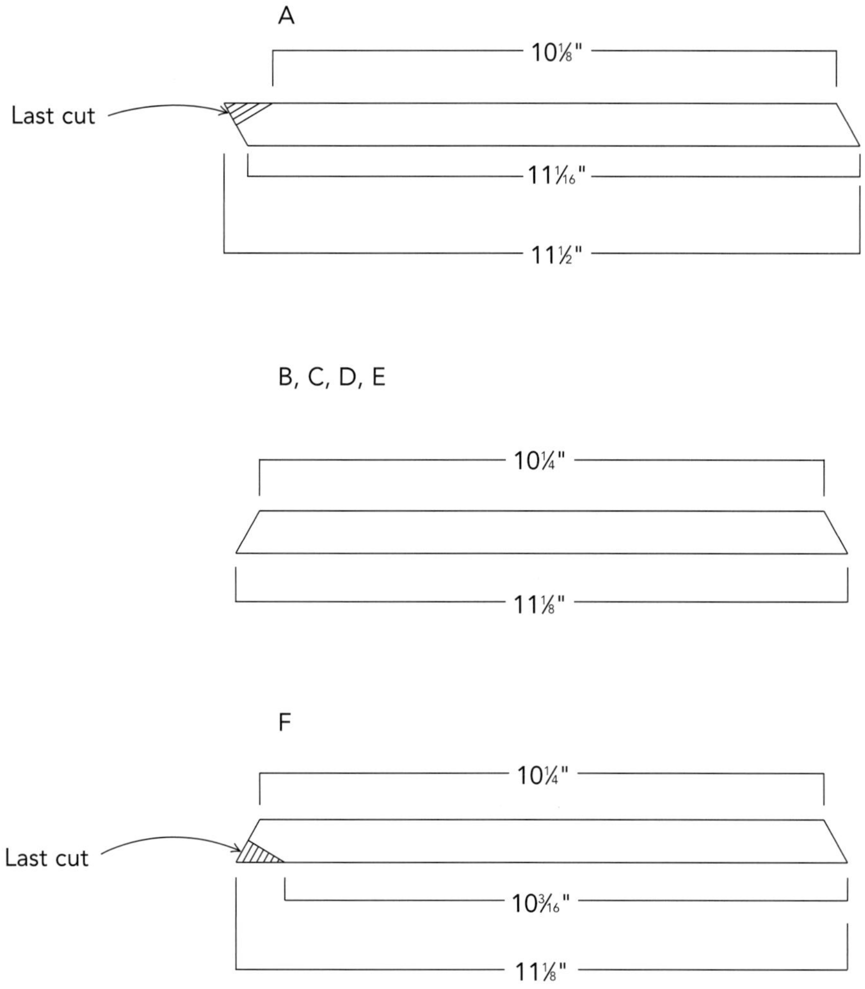

A
10⅛"
Last cut
11 1⁄16"
11½"
B, C, D, E
10¼"
11⅛"
F
10¼"
Last cut
10 3⁄16"
11⅛"

change. You can see the potential nightmare of adding $\frac{5}{32}$ in. to each partition and trying to cut something like a 58¼-degree angle.

Cutting the Sides and Partitions to Size

So here we go! The first step is to cut all the plywood parts.

1. Cut all the parts to the widths given in the cut list, leaving all the parts about 2 in. too long. The sides for the box are ¾ in. wider than the partitions because the partitions are inset front and back by as much.

2. Mill enough solid-mahogany edging stock to cover the front and back edges of all the parts.

3. Glue and clamp this edging to all these edges and set them aside to dry. It's easiest to leave this edging a little wide and long, so you can trim it flush after the glue has dried. This kind of edging is difficult to align perfectly, so if you leave some extra and it slides a little while being clamped, it will still cover the edges. When these parts are dry, trim all the edging flush with the faces of the plywood.

4. First trim the excess off the ends. This can be done very quickly by crosscutting ¼ in. or so off each end, which should still leave about 1½ in. of extra length.

5. Trim the excess from the sides. The quickest way to accomplish this is with a flush-trimming bit in your router. As long as you haven't left too much extra, you shouldn't have any splintering problems. You could also use a sharp block plane or even a sanding block. Regardless of the method you use, make sure that the edging ends up completely flush and level with the sides. If there is any rounding, it will show where all the parts come together.

Building the Box

It's hard to get out of the rut of measuring outside dimensions, but the most important thing to remember for this project is that the inside measurements are what count. I have also given you outside measurements for this wine rack, but these assume that the plywood you are using is exactly ¾ in. thick. As you may or may not know, ¾-in. plywood is rarely exactly ¾ in. and can be as much as 1⁄16 in. under. If you multiply this by two (the number of sides), you can make a box with interior dimensions as much as ⅛ in. off, more than enough to throw off the fit of the partitions. Other than that, it's just a box put together with biscuits.

1. Size the sides, top, and bottom for a box with inside dimensions of 33¼ in. by 9⅝ in., factoring in any stock-thickness variations.

2. Cut the biscuit slots so that the top and bottom are between the sides when assembled.

3. Finish-sand the inside faces of the box parts to 150 grit.

4. Glue, biscuit, and clamp the parts together. Make sure the box is still a true rectangle when clamped up.

5. When the glue is dry, finish-sand the outside.

Making the Feet

The box has four feet, attached with some brass screws over the plywood edges that show on the top and bottom of the box. Not only will these cover the raw plywood edges, but they also lift the bottom of the box slightly.

1. Mill four pieces of mahogany 12 in. by ⅜ in. by 13⁄16 in. for the feet.

2. Drill three countersunk holes, sized to brass screws at even intervals in each foot.

Making the Partitions

This part is not difficult, nor will it take very long, but you must be accurate (see "Summary of Cutting Sequence for Partitions" on p. 46).

1. Set the blade on your table saw to 60 degrees.

Summary of Cutting Sequence for Partitions

All cuts are made on the table saw.

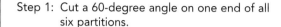

Step 1: Cut a 60-degree angle on one end of all six partitions.

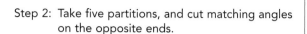

Step 2: Take five partitions, and cut matching angles on the opposite ends.

Step 3: Take the remaining partition, and cut a complementary 60-degree angle on its opposite end.

Step 4: Take the piece from Step 3. Using an angle-block carrier, hold the piece at 60 degrees to the blade, and cut the end off.

Step 5: Take one of the pieces from Step 2. Using an angle-block carrier, hold the piece at 60 degrees to the blade, and cut the end off.

PHOTO A: Cut 60-degree angles on the ends of every partition.

2. Set the fence so that each cut will take off about ⅛ in. to ¼ in. more than you need. This will ensure a splinter-free cut.

3. Rip a 60-degree angle on one end of all six of the partitions (see **photo A**).

4. Reset the fence to 11⅛ in., and rip a matching 60-degree angle on the opposite end of five of the six partitions. The same face of the partition should ride on the table during the cut.

5. Attach an auxiliary fence that sits perfectly flush with the table, and set the fence to cut at 11½ in. This auxiliary fence must lay tight to the table surface. The next cut requires that the long point of the last partition rides on the table and against the fence. You don't want any space under the rip fence under which the point could slip.

6. Cut a complementary 60-degree angle without a bevel on the end of the last partition (see **photo B**). (This partition is shown as "A" in "Exact Partition Sizes" on p. 44.)

7. Make an angle-block carrier to hold the top and bottom partitions ("A" and "F" on p. 44) at 60 degrees to the sawblade. This allows you to cut the secondary angles that are at 90 degrees to the 60-degree angles. A simple block of wood about 18 in. long by 1¾ in. high by 2½ in. wide will work fine (see "Positioning Angle-Block Carrier").

8. Attach one of the two partitions to this block with some double-sided tape. (Both of these partitions will be cut the same way, with the same exact setup.)

PHOTO B: Cut a complementary 60-degree angle on the ends of the top partition ("A" on p. 44).

Positioning Angle-Block Carrier

Partition

Rip fence

Angle-block carrier, 1¾" high x 2½" wide x 18" long

Sawblade

Offcut

Distance from fence to sawblade is 1¹⁵⁄₁₆".

PHOTO C: An auxiliary block angles the top and bottom partitions to cut the corners of one edge at 90 degrees to the 60-degree bevel.

9. With the blade at 90 degrees to the table, set the rip fence 1¹⁵⁄₁₆ in. away from the blade. Then run the partition through (see **photo C**). Repeat the procedure for the other partition. (Use "Exact Partition Sizes" on p. 44 to check that you've got your angles oriented properly.)

Assembly

Before you glue the partitions in place, do a dry assembly to check the fit.
1. Stand the box on end.
2. Starting at the bottom, place the partitions in the box one on top of the other (see **photo D**).

The accumulating weight of the partitions will spread the sides of the box a little, which is good since it will allow room for the last partition to be inserted. However, it will make it look as though nothing fits right, since the partitions are settling toward the bottom of the box. Don't worry.
3. Take some clamps and, working from the bottom up, position them front and back across the box at the joint of each partition.

PHOTO D: As you stack the partitions in the box, the sides will bow a little bit, making it easy to insert the top partition.

4. Lightly tighten the clamps as you go until the partitions fill up the space. If all the partitions have been cut correctly, they will lie nicely one on top of the other with all the intersecting joints tight.
5. Just to be sure, check that the box is the same width in the center as it is at the top and at the bottom; also, check the diagonals to be sure it is square.
6. Once you are satisfied with the fit, remove the partitions and finish-sand them to 150 grit.

7. Starting at the bottom again, carefully apply a light bead of glue down the center of each end of the first partition and place it in the box. Remember that the partitions are set in ⅜ in. front and back from the edges of the box. Make sure to keep glue away from the last inch or so of the edge at the front and back. This will be plenty of glue to hold things together, and this way it shouldn't make a mess (which otherwise would be very difficult to clean up).

8. Continue gluing and installing partitions until they are all in. The box should spread a little like before, and you should have no problem getting the top partition in without smearing glue on the inside of the box. If it's tight, just spread the sides a little with your hands and it should be fine.

9. Clamp it up just as you did during the dry assembly and check for square (see **photo E**). That's it!

Finishing

This is a very difficult piece to spray finish (or oil for that matter). The compartments created by the partitions make it difficult to get the finish inside. But like an old cabinetmaker I used to know once said, it's also difficult for anyone to see if it's finished in there! So I ended up spraying it the best I could with some satin lacquer. It looks fine—but don't you dare pull out a bottle just to see how well it's finished inside.

PHOTO E: Clamp the case sides together at each partition joint, both front and back. The clamping will make the top partition joint snug.

SPICE AND TEA SHELF

WHEN COLLECTING PROJECTS for this book, I just had to include this shelf. There has been an almost identical one in my kitchen for many years, and I wouldn't think of doing without it. I happened upon it before I became a woodworker, in a gift store, hanging on a wall and filled with mugs. I'm not sure exactly why I was so attracted to it, but I just had to have it. When I asked about it, the store owner informed me that it was only part of the display. Not one to be put off when I want something, I pushed the issue and was rewarded: The manager ordered one for me. Unfortunately, I had no good use for it.

As it turns out, the shelf has been one of the most useful kitchen storage items I've ever had. At the time, I lived in a tiny apartment in Brooklyn, New York, which had almost no free wall space. By default, the shelf ended up on a small sliver of wall space next to the stove. Slowly but surely, the shelf filled with the things I used near the stove (what a surprise!): spices, condiments, containers of tea and coffee, etc. Unlike other so-called spice racks, this shelf holds a fair amount of stuff. When I moved to another apartment with no similar wall space near the stove, I discovered that this shelf works just as well horizontally.

Made of stained pine stapled together, the original shelf was unremarkable, except for its long and seemingly thin proportions. The shape makes this piece both pleasing to the eye and useful in the kitchen. The version in this chapter is slightly longer, wider, and deeper than the one I bought close to 30 years ago. The larger size more easily accommodates items such as tea boxes and larger spice containers. I made it from walnut rather than the original pine.

SPICE AND TEA SHELF

This long, thin shelf provides valuable open storage in a kitchen—perfect for tea, coffee, spices, and other sundries.

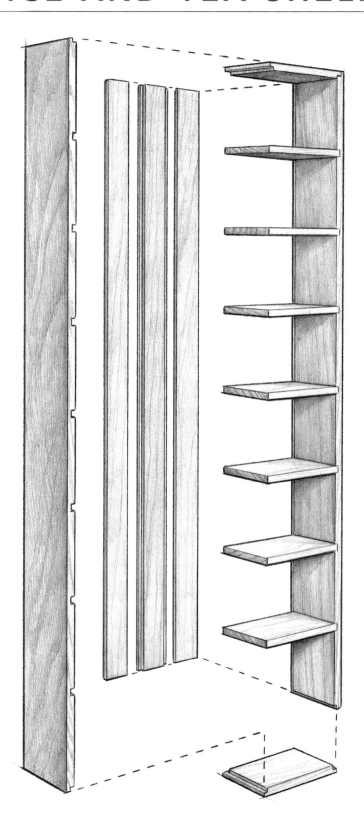

Front and Side Views

FRONT

SIDE

50½"

5¾"

6"

3¼"

6½"

3½"

Construction and Assembly

I CHOSE WALNUT FOR THIS PROJECT because I thought that a hardwood would be a better choice than soft pine. The walnut also most closely matches the dark stain of the old shelf, which proved to be a good choice for a kitchen environment. The joinery is very simple and so is the setup. Once you have the pieces milled to size, the rest of the work is on the table saw. It's important that all the parts are the same thickness (except the back) to ensure that the joints are tight.

1. Mill the shelves, sides, and top and bottom to precisely ½ in. thick.

2. Cut them to their finished size, according to the dimensions in the cut list. Keep the cutoffs to use later for test pieces.

Cutting the Joinery

All of the joinery is easily cut on the table saw, with the same ½-in. dado blade installed for all steps. Adding a simple auxiliary fence makes it possible to use the same blade for different-width cuts without changing the setup or cutting into your rip fence.

Rabbets for the sides, back, and top

The rabbets along the back edges of the sides, top, and bottom capture the back. The rabbets on the ends of these pieces make up the corner joints of the case.

1. Install a ½-in.-wide dado blade in the table saw.

2. Make and attach a piece of medium-density fiberboard (MDF) or scrap plywood, at least ¾ in. thick, to the face of the rip fence. This will serve as an auxiliary fence.

3. With the blade below the table surface, set the auxiliary fence ⅜ in. over the blade. Turn the saw on, and slowly raise the blade into the fence until the blade is ¼ in. high.

4. Set the fence to cut a ¼-in.-wide rabbet.

CUT LIST FOR SPICE AND TEA SHELF

2	Sides	50½" x 3½" x ½"	solid walnut
2	Top and bottom	6" x 3½" x ½"	solid walnut
7	Shelves	6" x 3¼" x ½"	solid walnut
1	Back	50" x 2⅛" x ¼"	solid walnut
2	Backs	50" x 2¹⁄₁₆" x ¼"	solid walnut

Other materials

25	Brass screws	#4 x ⅝"

Cutting the shelf dadoes in the sides

1. Without changing the height of the blade, reposition the rip fence 6¼ in. away from the dado blade.

2. With the end of the workpiece registering against the rip fence, and guiding the workpiece with the miter gauge, cut a dado on the inside face.

3. Spin the workpiece end for end, and repeat the process on the other end. Do this for both side pieces.

4. Cut the other shelf dadoes in the same way, repositioning the rip fence to make the dadoes evenly spaced (see "Dado Spacing").

5. The last dadoes you cut have to be in the very center of their respective sides. If they aren't, they won't line up (see **photo B**).

5. Rabbet the ends of the sides, top, and bottom, guiding them with the miter gauge, registering the ends against the auxiliary fence (see **photo A**).

6. Rabbet the back edge of the sides, top, and bottom by running them along the rip fence.

PHOTO A: Use both the rip fence and miter gauge to guide the rabbet cuts on the ends of the sides, top, and bottom.

Dado Spacing

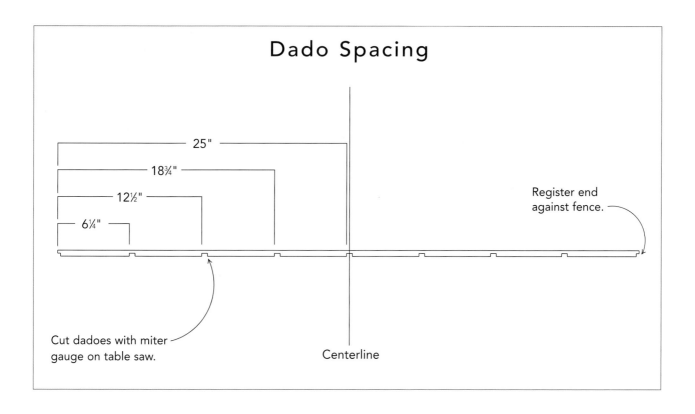

25"

18¾"

12½"

6¼"

Register end against fence.

Cut dadoes with miter gauge on table saw.

Centerline

PHOTO B: Cut the center dado of both sides last. Register the same end of each side against the rip fence to ensure the dadoes are aligned.

Assembling the Sides and Shelves

1. Sand all the parts to 150 grit. I recommend sanding by hand with a block. If you sand the shelves too much, they won't fit their dadoes.

2. Test-fit and match the shelves to dadoes for the best fit. Then label the shelves so they're easy to locate during glue-up.

3. Test assemble the case. Make any minor adjustments necessary.

4. Apply glue in the dadoes with a brush, covering the bottoms and the walls. Applying glue only in the dadoes will greatly reduce squeeze-out, which would be difficult to clean up.

5. Clamp up the shelf to a flat surface, such as a benchtop. Under clamping pressure, the thin wood can distort easily, making the fit of the dadoes either too loose or too tight, bowing the finished shelf. Make sure to apply clamping pressure across the length of each joint.

6. Check frequently for square as you apply clamps, and skew them as necessary to bring the joints square.

7. Clamp the top and bottom in place last, both to the bench and across the length of the shelf.

Attaching the Back

While the carcase dries, work on the back. You could make the back out of plywood; however, since I didn't have a piece of ¼-in. walnut plywood, I made a three-piece, shiplapped, solid-wood back. This configuration accommodates seasonal wood movement (see **photo C**).

1. Mill and size the three back pieces to finished dimensions (see "Thin Stock Options"). The piece in the center is a little wider.

2. Lower the dado blade to ⅛ in. high, then reset the rip fence to make a ³⁄₁₆-in.-wide cut.

3. Cut the rabbets in the back pieces. The center piece is rabbeted along both edges.

PHOTO C: The pieces for the back are shiplapped to accommodate seasonal wood movement.

THIN STOCK OPTIONS

Small projects often call for stock thinner than standard ¾ in. The thinner stock can give the piece a lighter look and rarely compromises strength. While you can certainly plane down 4/4 stock to ½ in. thick, you'll end up wasting 50 percent of the board feet you just bought. Alternatively, you can buy thin stock from some mail-order catalogs (see Resources), but you are limited in size, selection, and species.

A better alternative is to resaw your own stock. The bandsaw is the very best tool for resawing. The thin blade wastes very little wood, and the throat capacity of even a small bandsaw is enough to make average widths of lumber. The table saw can also be used to

resaw but is limited by the cutting height, and the wider blade wastes more stock. In my opinion, it's also risky to resaw on the table saw.

Resawn on the bandsaw, lumber that's about 1 in. thick will yield two ⅜-in.-thick boards. To get ½-in.-thick lumber through resawing, you need to start with pieces at least 1¼ in. thick. Resawing often releases tensions in the wood, causing it to distort. The extra thickness is needed to straighten out the boards and obtain ½-in.-thick finished pieces.

Resawing is also the way to achieve book-matched boards. Glued together, they can make distinctive panels for cabinets and doors.

The two other pieces are rabbeted only along the inside edge (see "Detail of Back" on p. 58).

4. Finish-sand the pieces to 150 grit.

5. Fit one of the side back pieces tight into the back of the case. Use a clamp if necessary.

6. Drill and countersink pilot holes along the edge, and screw into the rabbet on the sides. Place the screws midway between each shelf. Make sure you properly size the pilot holes. The hole should be slightly bigger than the width of the screw shank. Brass is very soft, and it's easy to break the screws when the holes are too small.

7. Repeat the process for the other side back piece. Note that there isn't much to screw into. Use small #4 brass screws, and angle the pilot hole very slightly.

8. Fit the center piece, spaced evenly between the two side pieces. Drill and countersink pilot holes into the center of the back of each shelf, as well as the top and bottom into the rabbet (see **photo D**).

PHOTO D: Screw the center back panel into the shelves. Treat the brass screws gently, as they break off easily.

Detail of Back

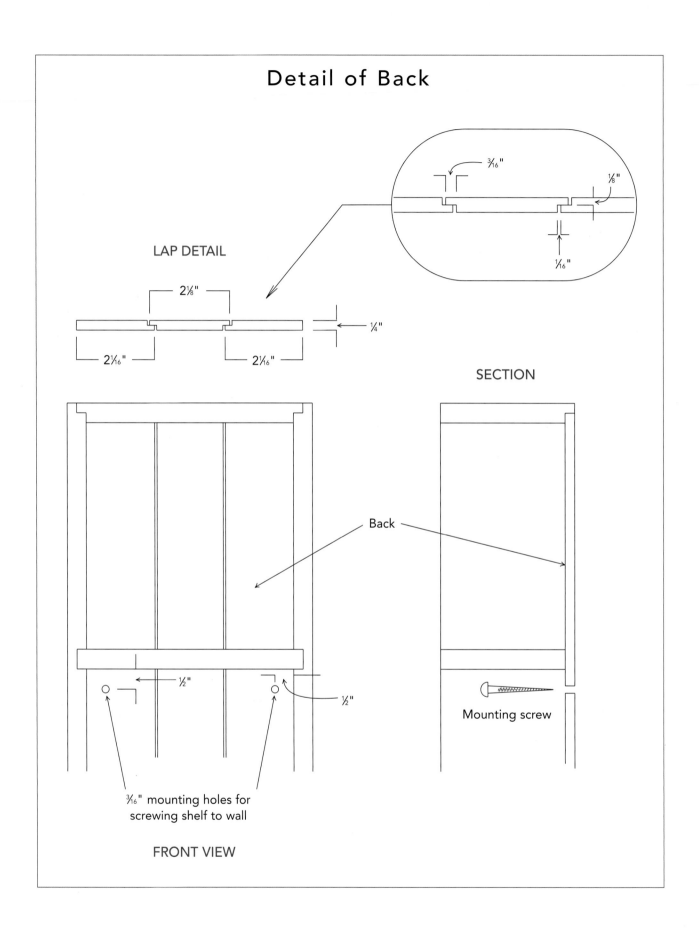

LAP DETAIL

3/16 "

1/8 "

1/16 "

2 1/8 "

1/4 "

2 1/16 "

2 1/16 "

SECTION

Back

Mounting screw

1/2 "

1/2 "

3/16 " mounting holes for
screwing shelf to wall

FRONT VIEW

DESIGN OPTION: HORIZONTAL SPICE SHELF

At over 4 ft. tall, this shelf can be difficult to place in a kitchen. There might not be a vertical space tall enough in your kitchen to accommodate it. The shelf works just fine, though, when hung horizontally.

The shelves become dividers, and the side on the top becomes a second shelf space. Also, you can make shorter (or taller) versions of this shelf, as you like.

Horizontally, the shelf offers two levels of storage space—in the shelves and on top.

Finishing Up

1. Drill four ³⁄₁₆-in. holes—two at each end—through the back at the locations shown (see "Detail of Back"). Only two on one end are necessary to hang the shelf vertically. The other two make it possible to hang the shelf in either a vertical orientation or a horizontal one (see "Design Option: Horizontal Spice Shelf").

2. Finish-sand the outside of the carcase to 150 grit.

3. Apply an oil finish. I used Watco Danish Oil, but any high-quality oil finish will work just fine. As not all oil finishes work in the same way, I recommend following the manufacturer's directions. I've never gone wrong this way.

PAPER-TOWEL HOLDER AND PINCHING TOWEL RACK

TOWELS, BOTH PAPER AND CLOTH, are necessities in the kitchen. Nothing beats a quick paper-towel snatch for those sudden spills that would send a cloth towel to the laundry. But using only paper towels is wasteful. Cloth towels are just the thing for drying your hands or those few items that shouldn't go in the dishwasher.

The trick is to keep cloth towels close at hand, without having them looped through the refrigerator-door handle or thrown over the back of a chair. Paper towels are a little easier since there are many holders one can buy, but most are clumsy to use or need to be screwed to the wall, making if difficult to bring the roll to the spill.

The two projects in this chapter will give you handy and attractive places to store both types of towels. The paper-towel holder is portable and easy to load, and allows you to snatch one towel without the whole roll following. The pinching towel rack is (if I do say so myself) a little more clever. The inspiration and basic principle came from some V-shaped, molded-plastic holders my wife and I brought back from a trip to Denmark. These particular holders work well, but they are not very pleasing to look at. They are also designed for single towels, and I wanted a rack that would hold at least a few.

PAPER-TOWEL HOLDER

The knob, post, top, and base are all octagonal in this simple holder.

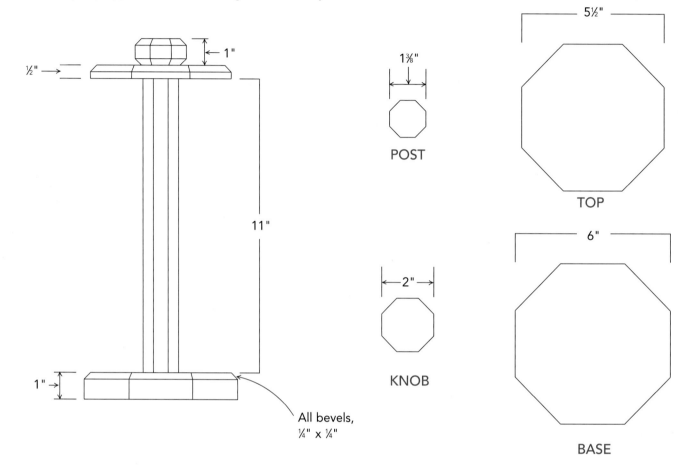

POST

1⅜"

5½"

TOP

KNOB

2"

6"

BASE

1"

½"

11"

1"

All bevels,
¼" x ¼"

CUT LIST FOR PAPER-TOWEL HOLDER

1	Knob	2" x 2" x 1"	solid oak
1	Post	1⅜" x 1⅜" x 11"	solid oak
1	Top	5½" x 5½" x ½"	solid oak
1	Base	6" x 6" x 1"	solid oak

Other materials

1	Birch dowel	⅜" dia. x 2"	
1	Threaded insert	#20 x ¼"	
1	Hanger bolt	1½"	

Construction and Assembly

THIS IS A VERY UNCOMPLICATED project. There are no round or curved parts to make, since everything—including the center post—is octagonal. It is made entirely on the table saw and can be easily completed in a day. The post is simply doweled to the base, and the top is held on with a knob that screws on and off with a threaded insert.

Making the Post

1. Mill the post to the dimensions in the cut list.

2. Draw an equilateral octagon on the end of the workpiece.

3. Tilt the blade on your table saw to 45 degrees.

4. On a right-tilting saw, position the rip fence to the left of the blade; on a left-tilting saw, position the rip fence to the right of the blade. This prevents the workpiece from being captured under the blade, making the cut safer.

5. Using the octagon on the end of the workpiece as a visual guide, set the rip fence to cut almost to the line.

6. Make a test cut and adjust the fence a little at a time, creeping up on the cut until the blade splits the layout line.

7. Rip all four corners to create an equilateral octagon (see **photo A**).

8. Return the blade to 90 degrees.

Shaping the Base, Top, and Knob

Though cutting an octagon is simply cutting the corners of a square, making one with perfectly equal sides is something of a challenge. On the table saw, the easiest way is to set a stop block on the miter gauge to position the workpiece so that all four corners can be cut the same. There's no good way to

PHOTO A: With the blade tilting at 45 degrees away from the fence, cut the four corners of the post blank to produce an equilateral octagon.

PHOTO B: A miter gauge and stop block ensure consistent facet lengths, both when cutting the sides and shaping the facets.

accurately set the block without trial and error. Just creep up on the perfect cut as you did with the post.

1. Mill the base, top, and knob to the dimensions in the cut list.

2. Lay out equilateral octagons on all three parts.

3. Set your table saw's miter gauge to 45 degrees.

4. Make a stop block at least 2½ in. square. This ensures it still registers against the workpiece during the final cut when there is no full corner.

5. To cut the facets on the base, position the workpiece against the miter gauge close to the line of cut. Hold it there.

6. Slide the stop block up against the edge of the workpiece that is away from the blade, and clamp it to the face of the miter gauge.

7. Make a test cut, then reset the block in small increments until you get a perfect facet.

8. Trim the other three corners.

9. Repeat the process for the top and the knob.

10. When cutting the knob, do not hold it in place with your fingers. I used double-sided tape on both the stop block and the miter gauge to hold the knob during the cut, which seemed to work just fine. However, never do anything that doesn't feel right.

11. Tilt the table-saw blade to 45 degrees.

12. Cut the ¼-in. bevels on the upper edge of the base and top and on both edges of the knob. Use the same setup and procedure as you did for shaping these parts (see **photo B**).

Assembly and Finishing

You will need a few items to finish assembling this piece. The first is a ⅜-in. dowel, which should be a proper dowel pin and not a piece of dowel rod. (A dowel pin is accurately machined and sized and has grooves or flutes in the sides to allow glue to escape the hole.) You will also need a threaded insert with a #20 by ¼-in. internal thread and a 1½-in. hanger bolt with matching thread. (Hanger bolts have wood-screw threads at one end and machine threads at the other.)

1. Drill ⅜-in.-dia. holes in the center of the base and in the center of each end of the post. Drill the hole in the base as deep as possible without going through—approximately ⅞ in. deep. Drill the holes in the post approximately 1¼ in. deep.

2. Drill a ¼-in.-dia. hole through the center of the top.

3. Drill a 3/16-in.-dia. hole in the center of the underside of the knob, approximately ¾ in. deep.

4. Finish-sand all the pieces to 150 grit.

5. Attach the post to the base with a ⅜-in. dowel glued in place. Be sure to line up the facets. Clamp and set aside until dry.

6. Set the threaded insert in the top hole in the post. There are different methods of setting inserts depending on the type you have; check with the supplier for details.

7. Screw the wood-screw end of the hanger bolt into the hole in the knob. (see **photo C**).

8. If you like, you can mark and cut a 1/16-in.-deep octagonal recess in the underside of the top to capture the post and align the facets of the top and base. I used a laminate trimmer to rout the recess, and cleaned up the corners with a chisel. This recess also shortens the post somewhat, thus clamping the towel-roll ends slightly; this helps to keep your kids from pulling every last towel off the roll in one pull.

PHOTO C: The knob secures the top to the post with a threaded insert and hanger bolt.

9. Apply the finish of your choice. I used an oil finish.

10. After the finish has dried, to put the towel rack to use, it's a simple matter of placing a roll of towels over the center post, lining up the top, and screwing down the knob.

PINCHING TOWEL RACK

Half disks attached to a back make this very simple and elegant rack. Wedging the corner of a towel down into one of the slots holds the towel firmly in place.

TOP VIEW

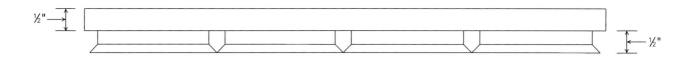

FRONT VIEW

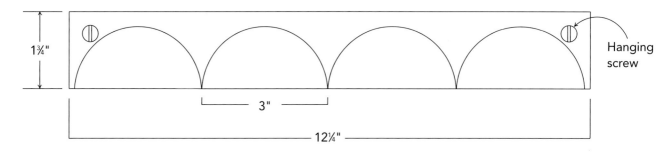

Hanging screw

CUT LIST FOR PINCHING TOWEL RACK			
1	Blank for disks	15" x 4" x ½"	curly maple
1	Blank for backs	12¼" x 3¾"x ½"	curly maple

Construction and Assembly

THE KEY TO THIS RACK is a thin, beveled edge that the corner of the towel can be wedged down into. To tell the truth, I had almost given up on finding a way to build this piece. Then, in the process of cutting some circles for another job, the proverbial lightbulb went on over my head. I looked at the cutter I was using and abandoned the idea of trying to make V-shaped wedges in favor of circular ones. Suddenly the project was not only possible but also easy.

The cutter (shown in **photo D**) can cut a circle with a small bevel at the outer edge—just the thing for pinching towels. This method of construction also makes two towel racks. Once the piece is cut and shaped, you'll have one rack to keep and one to give to a good friend on a special occasion.

Shaping and Assembly

1. Mill the blanks for the back and the disks to the dimensions in the cut list.

2. Install a circle cutter, available from many woodworking-tool suppliers (see Resources), in a drill press with the cutter oriented as shown in **photo D**.

3. Set the drill-press speed to around 720 rpm. Make a test cut in a piece of scrap. If the cutter is running too fast, it will burn the workpiece. If it is running too slow, it will chatter in the cut. Adjust until the cutter produces a clean, finished cut.

4. Clamp the disk blank to the drill-press table.

5. Cut four 3-in.-dia. circles out of the disk blank (see **photo D**).

6. Draw a line along the center of the back.

7. Drill ⅛-in.-dia. pilot holes 3⅛ in. from one end and then evenly spaced 3 in. apart from there. These will help locate the disks on the back.

8. Finish-sand all the parts to 150 grit.

9. Apply a light film of glue to the center of the disks, staying at least ½ in. from the edges. You don't want any glue squeeze-out because it's extremely difficult to clean out.

10. Align and apply the disks to the back, so that their center holes are aligned over the pilot holes in the back and their edges just touch.

11. Screw the disks to the back through their center holes. You should not need to clamp the disks to the back.

12. When dry, remove the screws. This is important to remember (you'll see why).

13. Set the rip fence on your table saw to 1¾ in.

14. Rip the assembly (see **photo E**). Rip the offcut to produce the second rack. Make sure that the center holes are completely removed.

15. Finish the rack however you like. I simply waxed this one with butcher's wax. It simplifies the finishing process greatly and leaves a nice sheen.

PHOTO D: With the blade positioned with the bevel facing inward, a common circle cutter cuts disks with a pinching bevel.

PHOTO E: Rip the blank to create two racks, and eliminate the drill holes in the center.

DISH-DRYING RACK

HAVE ALWAYS LIKED THE NOTION of dish racks. Traditionally hung over a sink, they not only provide storage space for your dishes but a place for them to drip dry. This makes it possible to put them away without bothering to wipe them. I have unfortunately never had a kitchen that allowed this use. The sinks in my kitchens have always been located in front of windows or beneath cabinets. Luckily, these racks are handsome enough to double as display racks to showcase your dinnerware, no matter where they are located.

When designing this piece I wanted to accomplish two things. I wanted it to have as large a holding capacity as possible and still fit comfortably between or next to upper cabinets. I also wanted it to be able to fit into any style kitchen, from contemporary to traditional.

At first glance, this dish rack may appear complicated and difficult to build. In reality, it is nothing more than three identically built frames screwed together, with two curved side supports screwed on last. Fabricating the laminated supports is relatively easy, once you have built the form. If you've never done this type of work before, this project will give you an extremely useful skill for other projects down the road.

The clean, vertical lines of this ash plate-drying rack will easily make it a welcome fixture in your kitchen. It will allow you dry or store up to 14 full-size dinner plates on the lower tier and an equal number of dessert plates or a mixture of cups and saucers or mugs on the upper tier.

DISH-DRYING RACK

This updated version of a drying rack will blend well in both modern and traditional kitchens. Three frames connect together and are supported by two curved arms.

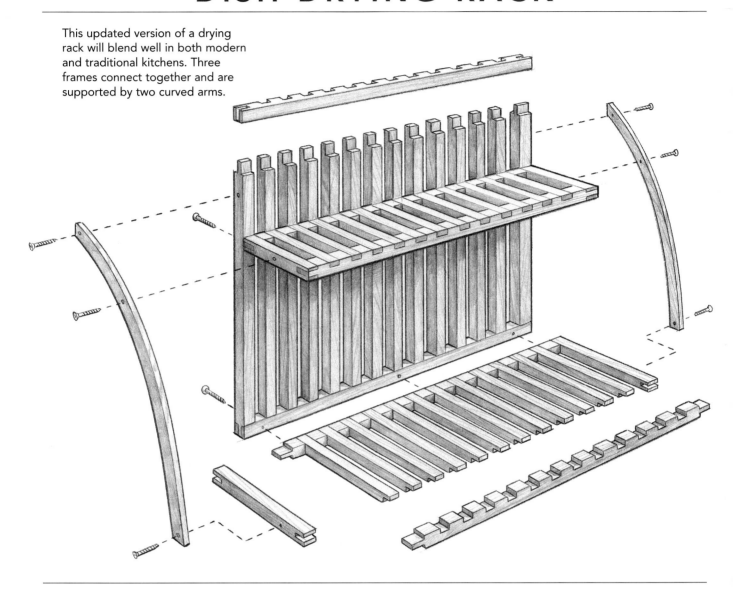

Milling the Straight Parts

DUE TO THE REPETITION OF joinery, the smart route is to cut joinery (rabbets and dadoes) in large boards, then rip them to size. Try to pick straight-grained, dry lumber. The less straightening you have to do to the individual parts (a total of 51), the better.

1. For the frame rails, mill a board at least 6 in. wide, ¾ in. thick, and 28¾ in. long.

2. For the slats and stiles, mill nine boards ¾ in. thick by 5 in. to 6 in. wide, at three different lengths: three boards 22 in. long, three 9 in. long, and three 6 in. long.

3. Rip two pieces ¾ in. wide off one of each board length. You want two pieces 22 in. long, two pieces 9 in. long, and two pieces 6 in. long. Set them to one side. These will become the stiles for the frame.

Front, Back, and Side Views

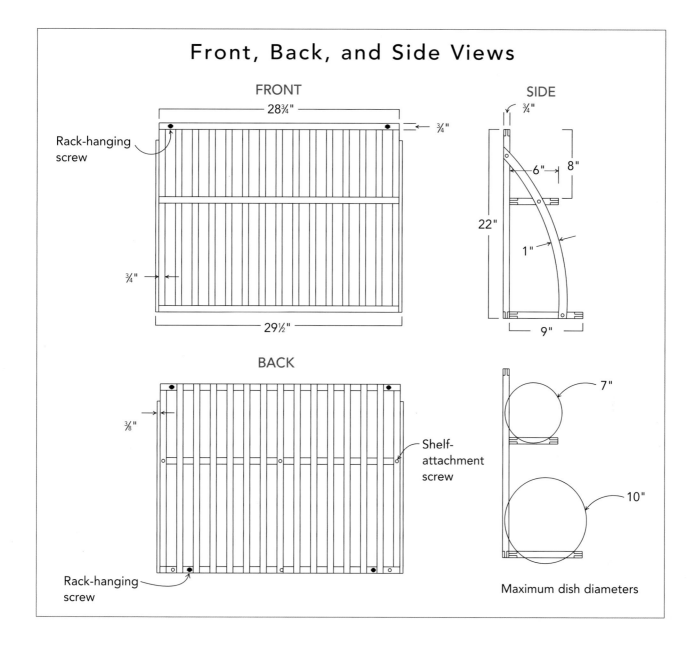

Maximum dish diameters

Cutting the Dadoes in the Rail Blank

1. Install a ¾-in.-wide dado blade in the table saw.
2. Position the rip fence 2 in. from the dado blade and set the blade exactly ½ in. high.
3. Guiding the rail blank with the miter gauge, and with the end of the workpiece registering against the rip fence, cut a dado.
4. Spin the workpiece end for end, and repeat the process.

5. Reposition the rip fence 3¼ in. away from the blade, and cut the next set of dadoes.
6. Repeat this process, repositioning the fence away from the dado blade in 2-in. increments until you've cut dadoes across the whole face of the board.

Cutting the Rabbets on the Slat Blanks

1. Make and add a ¾-in.-thick auxiliary fence to your table saw's rip fence. A piece of plywood or other scrap is fine. The auxiliary

CUT LIST FOR DISH-DRYING RACK			
6	Rails	¾" x ¾" x 28¾"	solid ash
2	Stiles, large frame	¾" x ¾" x 22"	solid ash
2	Stiles, lower shelf	¾" x ¾" x 9"	solid ash
2	Stiles, upper shelf	¾" x ¾" x 6"	solid ash
13	Slats, large frame	¾" x ¾" x 22"	solid ash
13	Slats, lower shelf	¾" x ¾" x 9"	solid ash
13	Slats, upper shelf	¾" x ¾" x 6"	solid ash
8	Laminate strips	1" x ⅛" x 36"	ash
Other materials			
6	Brass screws	#6 x ¾"	
6	Wood screws	#6 x 1½"	
4	Rubber bumpers, clear	⅛" thick	

fence keeps your dado blade from cutting into your rip fence.

2. Position the rip fence so that it just barely touches the dado blade. You want the rabbet just ¾ in. wide.

3. Cut the ½-in.-deep rabbet on both ends of the nine slat blanks (see **photo A**).

Ripping the Rails and Slats to Size

You'll want to rip the rail and slat pieces a bit wide, so that the saw marks will be easy to clean up. Also, if the pieces warp a little, you can straighten them out without milling them undersize.

PHOTO A: Cut the rabbets in the ends of the slat blanks, using the miter gauge to guide the piece and the rip fence to set the width of the cut. Use the same method to dado the rails.

PHOTO B: Rip the dadoed rail and slat blanks at the same time and to the same width (13⁄16 in.).

1. Remove the dado blade from the saw, and install a rip blade.

2. Rip the nine slat and rail blanks into $^{13}/_{16}$-in.-wide pieces (see **photo B**).

3. Joint and then plane the sawn faces to a finished width of ¾ in., exactly the width of the dadoes in the rails. It's fine if some pieces have a little warp.

Cutting the Bridle Joints for the Frame

You should cut the mortise members in the rails first, because it's easier to fit the tenons to the mortises than the other way around (see "Joinery Details").

1. Cut the open mortises, ¾ in. deep and ¼ in. wide, centered on the ends of the rails. I use a simple shopmade jig for this work (see **photo C** and the photo on p. 11), which

PHOTO C: Using a table saw and jig, cut the bridle joints. Either a shopmade or a commercial jig will work fine.

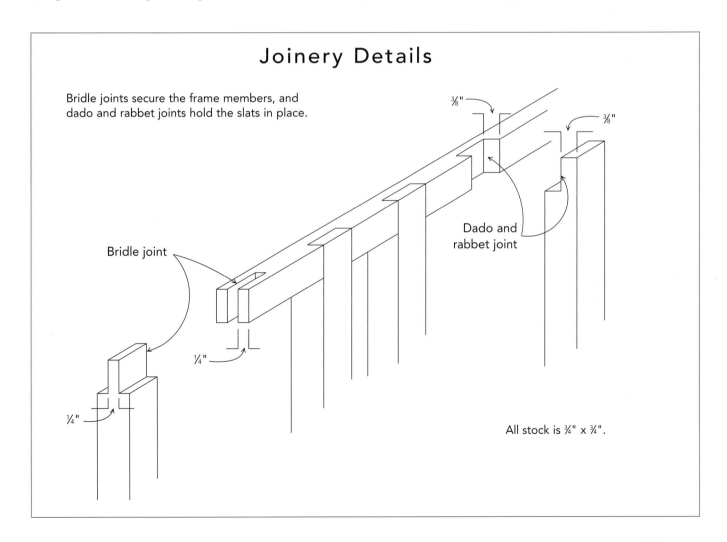

Joinery Details

Bridle joints secure the frame members, and dado and rabbet joints hold the slats in place.

⅜"

⅜"

Dado and rabbet joint

Bridle joint

¼"

¼"

All stock is ¾" x ¾".

PHOTO D: Cut the tenon shoulders on the table saw, using the miter gauge to guide the workpiece through the cut and a stopped auxiliary fence to make the shoulder locations consistent. The auxiliary fence should end before the blade cuts into the workpiece.

PHOTO E: Glue and clamp the frames together, making sure the bridle joints are snug. Then add slats as many at a time as you have clamps.

supports the workpiece vertically on the table saw.

2. Cut the tenon faces, ¾ in. deep, in the ends of the stiles, using the same jig on the table saw (see **photo C** on p. 73).

3. Cut the tenon shoulders using the miter gauge to guide the workpiece (see **photo D**).

Assembling Three Frames

1. Assemble the rails and stiles of the three frames, gluing and clamping the bridle joints.

2. Clamp the joints across the width and length of the frame to bring the shoulders of the joints together. Clamp as near to the joint as possible without interfering with the joint closing.

3. Now, clamp the joints across their faces. At this point, you can remove the other clamps. Wait until the glue has set before going on to the next step (installing the slats).

4. For the first slat, brush a little glue on the bottom and sides of the dadoes in the rails. This should be enough to hold it in place without a lot of glue squeeze-out, which would be hard to clean out between the slats.

5. One by one, install each slat and clamp it in place. You don't have to install all of them at once, since it takes 26 clamps for all the slats in each frame (see **photo E**).

6. When the glue has cured, clean up the frames and finish-sand them to 150 grit.

Making the Curved Support Arms

The curved support arms are bent laminations. It's a relatively simple process, though you'll need to build a jig.

1. Build a laminating jig, made from two layers of ¾-in. plywood (see "Bent Lamination Form").

2. Rip eight ⅛-in.-thick pieces 1 in. wide and 36 in. long. Ripping such thin pieces on

BENT LAMINATION FORM

The bent lamination form is made very simply from two sheets of plywood, with a 1-in. curved groove routed in the first layer.

1. Screw together two 9-in. by 34-in.-pieces of ¾-in. plywood, face to face. Place the screws in the locations indicated on the drawing to prevent routing through a screw later.
2. Set up a router trammel jig, either commercial or shopmade will work equally well, and fit your router with a ¾-in. straight plunge bit.
3. Rout the 23½-in. outside radius, ¾ in. deep. Make several light passes at partial depth so as to not strain the bit.
4. Rout the inside radius at 22½ in. Be careful to move the router in the direction that makes the bit rotate into the cut. If you move the router in the opposite direction, the bit may self-feed and pull the router out of your hands.

5. Remove the screws and separate the parts of the jig.
6. Apply clear packing tape to the edges of the cauls and the base of the groove. The tape prevents the laminations from sticking to the form during glue-up.
7. Screw the concave caul back to the base.

A router trammel jig, whether commercial or shopmade, cuts the shape of the bending forms cleanly and easily.

Bent Lamination Form

9"

6"

Form is made from two layers of ¾" plywood, but only the top layer is routed.

34"

Location of screw connecting form layers

Radius 22½"

4"

Radius 17½"

Radius 23½"

1"

1"

Block, 1½" thick, raises trammel to the same height as form.

6"

Router trammel pivot point

PHOTO F: With the strips glued and stacked together and in the form, draw the concave and convex portions together with clamps. Check that the form and the strips lie flat, or the strut will set with a twist.

the table saw can lead to severe kickback. The safest way to do this is to start with a 1-in.-thick board at least 6 in. wide, rip oversize strips from the offcut edge, and then plane them to ⅛ in. thick.

3. Lay out seven of the eight pieces, and roll yellow glue on one face of each piece. In this application, I used polyvinyl acetate (PVA). It's fast and easy, and is appropriate for this project because the piece isn't bent to a very tight radius, there are no voids, and it won't undergo much stress in use.

4. Stack the seven pieces, glue side up, then put the eighth on top.

5. Place the lamination on the form between the convex and concave side. Squeeze the laminate between the sides of the form, flat against the base.

6. Clamp across the center of the form to draw the sides and laminate tight together. Add clamps across the rest of the form (see **photo F**). Make sure that the lamination and convex side of the form lie flat against the base.

7. When the glue has dried (at least overnight), remove the lamination from the form, and joint one edge, flattening it and cleaning off the glue squeeze-out.

8. Rip the lamination in half on the table saw. Do this carefully, keeping the jointed side against the rip fence and the convex side of the curve flat against the table next to the blade. This takes a continuous and curving motion, using a push stick to push the end of the lamination past the blade. If you're not comfortable doing this procedure on the table saw, either use a bandsaw or laminate two supports.

9. Plane the two pieces to ⅜ in. thick.

10. Finish-sand the arms to 150 grit.

Assembly and Finishing

1. Drill pilot holes through the back frame for the screws (locations shown in the drawings on p. 71).

2. Screw the lower shelf to the back frame flush with the bottom and sides.

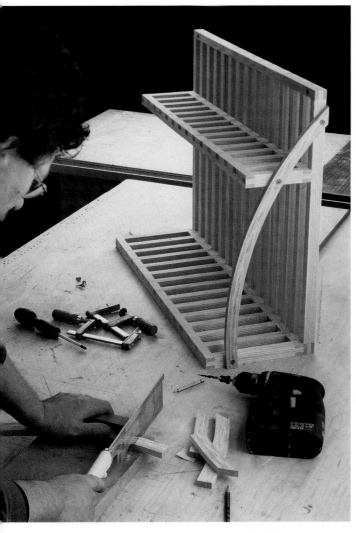

PHOTO G: After laying out the ends of the support arms, trim them to length and screw them in place.

Hanging Detail

Screws are located for easy access from front of rack.

Top screws are decorative brass. Install them straight into the wall.

Bottom screws are plain, installed at an angle between slats, and are hidden.

3. Screw the upper shelf to the back frame 8 in. from the top.

4. Mark the locations for the support arms on the edges of the frames, and hold the arms in place. Then mark where you need to trim the ends of the arms to fit.

5. Cut the ends of the arms (see **photo G**).

6. Drill and countersink the arms, and screw them to the back and to the upper and lower frames.

7. Apply the finish of your choice to the rack. I used an oil finish, which is easy to apply to all the many, little parts.

8. When the finish is dry, attach four ⅛-in.-thick rubber bumpers to the back of the frame. This pushes the frame out from the wall a little and keeps very large plates from hitting the wall.

9. Drill pilot holes for the hanging screws (locations shown in the drawings on p. 71).

10. The specific length of the screws you use to hang the rack depends on the wall you're screwing into (see "Hanging Detail"). Try to choose attractive screws because they will show in the finished rack.

SERVING TRAY AND LAZY SUSAN

WHO HAS NOT RELISHED the idea of being served breakfast or at least afternoon tea? Imagine a tray bearing delicious things to eat, freshly squeezed fruit juices, and maybe even the clichéd single rose in a vase.

Serving trays, such as the one presented here, carry an air of luxury and a refined sense of convenience about them. Unlike times past, most of us do our own serving these days, but the ritual remains the same. In addition, these trays are useful when entertaining. Carrying a pot of tea and cups to the living room, or even clearing plates after dinner, is made a lot easier with a serving tray such as this.

Compared to the traditional serving tray, the lazy Susan is a more modern notion of convenience. Like the serving tray, its job is to transport food objects conveniently and with ease. What better place for

food to congregate than the center of the table? And what could be more useful than a turntable that allows you to retrieve condiments without instituting a sort of condiment brigade around the table?

As projects go, these two are deceptively simple. Neither will take very much time to make, but they each present a certain amount of technical difficulty. The tray requires some precision cutting for the joinery, and it's a bit tricky to clamp up. The laminated rim of the lazy Susan requires about six hands and a good deal of luck to get right. And, to be honest, it may not work on the first try.

The good news is that I have already made most of the mistakes there are to make on these two projects, and my warnings should help you avoid them. After all, that's what I am here for!

SERVING TRAY

This elegant serving tray uses a variation on
the box joint, with routed handle openings
on the sides.

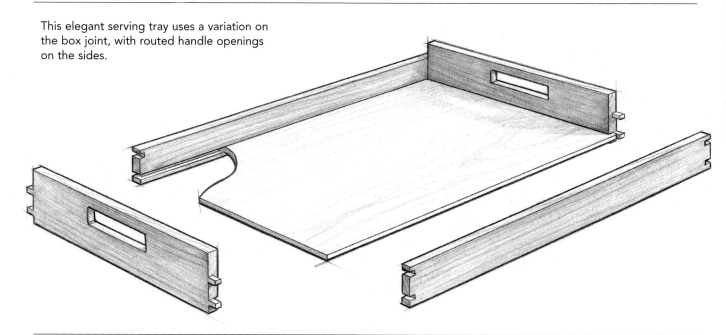

Side, Top, and End Views

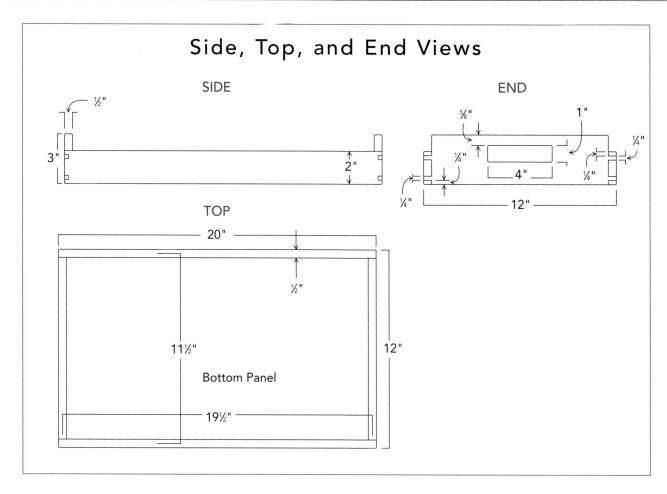

CUT LIST FOR SERVING TRAY

2	Long tray sides	20" x 2" x ½"	solid mahogany
2	Short tray sides	12" x 3" x ½"	solid mahogany
1	Tray bottom	11½" x 19½" x ¼"	mahogany plywood

Construction and Assembly

MADE THIS TRAY OUT OF mahogany because I like this wood and I had a piece of ¼-in. mahogany plywood left over from another job. It may not be the easiest material to find, especially the relatively small piece you will need for the bottom of this tray. There is certainly no reason why you can't use a wood more to your liking and perhaps one that's easier to obtain.

Cutting a Groove for the Bottom

1. Mill the solid-wood parts for the sides to the dimensions stated in the cut list.

2. Cut a piece of ¼-in. plywood for the bottom to the dimensions stated in the cut list. You will need to have the material for the bottom on hand to check the size of the groove it fits into.

3. Install a ¼-in. dado blade on your table saw, and set it to cut a groove ¼ in. deep, ¼ in. from the bottom of the workpiece.

4. Make a test cut in a piece of scrap wood to make sure the setup is correct. Check the fit of your plywood bottom panel in this test groove. It should be snug without needing to be forced. If it's too tight, you may have to shim your dado blade.

5. Once you are certain the setup is correct, cut a groove in the bottom inside face of each of the sides.

6. Leave the table saw as is. The setup for grooving the sides is the same for the first step in the joint sequence.

Cutting the Joints for the Long Sides

1. Build a jig or carrier that will hold the frame parts on end while you cut the corner joints (see "Carrier Jig" on p. 82). The jig is nothing more than a right angle of plywood with a support behind the face, which also acts as a handle to push the workpiece and jig through the table-saw blade while keeping your hand in a safe place.

Be sure to locate the screws that hold the jig together so that they will not be in the path of the blade when the jig is in use.

2. Without changing the table-saw dado setup, place the carrier jig against the rip fence.

PHOTO A: A simple carrier jig supports the long tray sides when notching the ends with a dado blade.

Carrier Jig

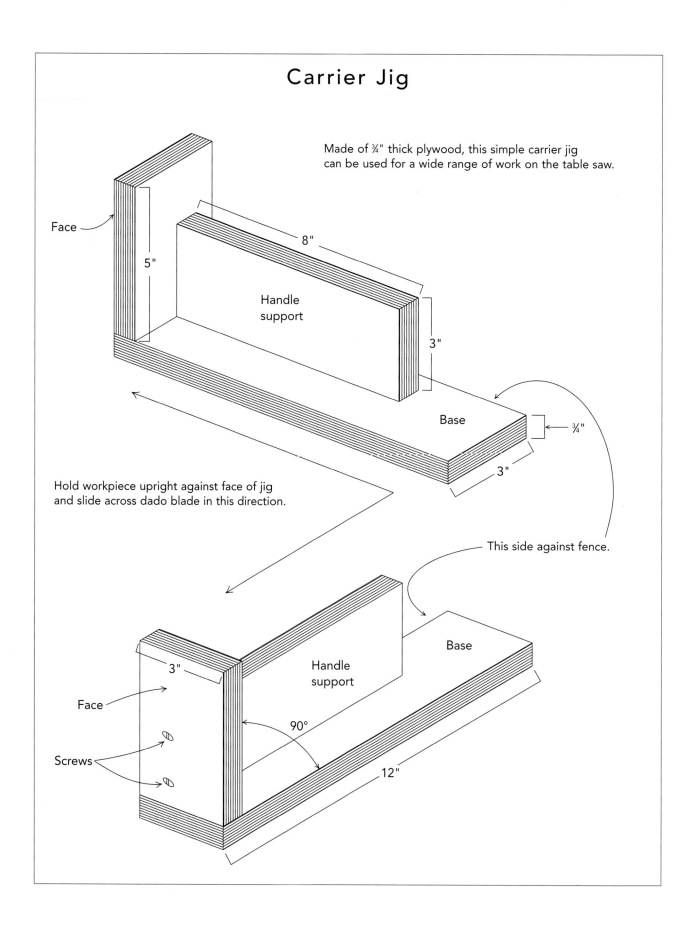

Made of ¾" thick plywood, this simple carrier jig can be used for a wide range of work on the table saw.

Face

5"

Handle support

8"

3"

Base

¾"

3"

Hold workpiece upright against face of jig and slide across dado blade in this direction.

This side against fence.

Face

3"

Handle support

Base

90°

Screws

12"

3. Position one of the long tray sides on end, flat against the face of the jig with the bottom-groove side against the fence. The groove will line up with the dado blade, and the slot you will cut here will be filled with a pin on the mating part of the joint hiding the groove.

4. Holding the workpiece in place, slide the jig across the dado blade (see **photo A** on p. 81).

5. Flip the workpiece so that the groove side is away from the fence, and repeat the cut.

6. Do the same for the other end of the workpiece and for both ends of the other long tray side. You'll end up with two notches in each end of the long sides, one in the same location as the groove for the bottom. This completes the joint work on these pieces.

Cutting the Joints for the Short Sides

The next step is to create pins on the ends of the short tray sides that fit the slots you made in the long tray sides. You will need to make five cuts in each end of the short pieces, but the saw settings are very simple.

1. With the same dado setup, and using your miter gauge set to 90 degrees, lay a short tray side inside face down with a long edge against the miter gauge.

2. Run the piece across the blade, nibbling away at the waste until the end meets the fence. This creates a ¼-in. by ½-in. rabbet in the end of the piece (see **photo B**).

3. Spin the piece around and cut a rabbet in the other end.

4. Repeat this procedure for the other short tray side.

5. Using the long sides as a template, mark the location of the pins with a sharp pencil or (better yet) a marking knife.

6. Raise your dado blade to ½ in. high. Using the marks you made on these parts as a reference, set your fence so that the dado blade is on one side of one pin and, using your carrier jig, make a cut in each end of

PHOTO B: With the same dado-blade setting, cut rabbets on the ends of the short tray sides.

PHOTO C: Cut away the waste around the marked pins, with the dado blade at the same setting as the last step.

PHOTO D: Crosscut the waste on the sides with the workpiece on edge. This leaves a cleaner finish on the ends.

each short tray side. Repeat this procedure to define the pins, then nibble away the waste between the pins (see **photo C** on p. 83).

7. Cut away the waste on the short ends to define what will be the handle portion of the tray ends (see **photo D** on p. 83). I do this work by crosscutting with the miter gauge rather than nibbling it away because this method leaves a better finish. (The end shows on the finished tray.) Raise the dado blade until it is just high enough to remove this waste, and set the fence so that it is just slightly more than ½ in. away from the outside of the blade.

It's a lot better to cut the shoulder just slightly smaller than exactly right. The slight reveal this creates is hardly noticeable, but it will assure that there is nothing in the way when you glue up the frame.

8. Make any adjustments necessary to fit the joints together. Remember, the pins are fragile, so don't force them.

Routing the Handle Opening

The handle opening is routed with a template and a plunge router fitted with a guide bushing and a straight plunge bit. The size of the template opening is determined by the diameter of the bit-and-bushing combination you use. Remember the smaller the bit and bushing you use, the smaller the radius in the corners of the cutout will be. I used a ⅛-in. bit with a ⁵⁄₁₆-in. bushing because I wanted as nearly square a cutout as possible.

1. Make the template (see "Handle-Routing Template").

2. Plunge and rout the hole in about three steps, going a little deeper each time. The tray sides are only ½ in. thick, but it is still a good idea. This is especially important if you are using a small-diameter bit, since these are fragile (see **photo E**).

PHOTO E: Plunge rout the handle hole in the sides with a template and collar guide.

Handle-Routing Template

The template is made of a frame that captures the workpiece, so no aligning is necessary from piece to piece. The workpiece is fitted into the template, and the template is screwed workpiece-side down to a piece of plywood clamped to the bench. This keeps the clamps out of the way of the routing operation.

SECTION THROUGH SIDE

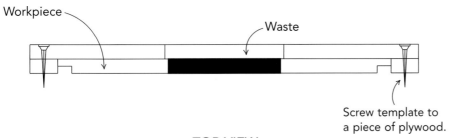

Workpiece

Waste

Screw template to a piece of plywood.

TOP VIEW

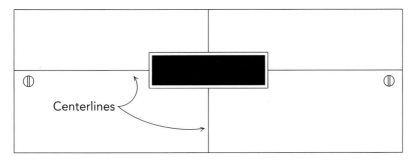

Centerlines

BOTTOM VIEW

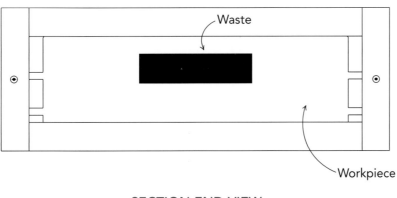

Waste

Workpiece

SECTION END VIEW

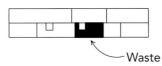

Waste

CUSTOM GLUE BLOCKS FOR CORNER JOINTS

Clamping corner joints such as dovetails and box joints can be tricky. Blocks on either side can prevent the joint from closing completely. The only other option is to clamp just to the side of the joint, which can distort the sides and leave the joints not quite bottomed out.

Instead, make some glue-up blocks or cauls that put pressure only where you want it. You'll need two different types of cauls. One will apply pressure to the pins, and the other will straddle the pins and apply pressure to the side.

Once you have the glue-up blocks prepared, try them out on the dry-assembled tray with some clamps, making sure all the joints close tightly. One last thing—you don't want the cauls to become glued to the joints. During clamp-up, cover their faces with some adhesive tape to keep them from sticking to the joints.

Similar blocks will work for dovetails and other types of box joints.

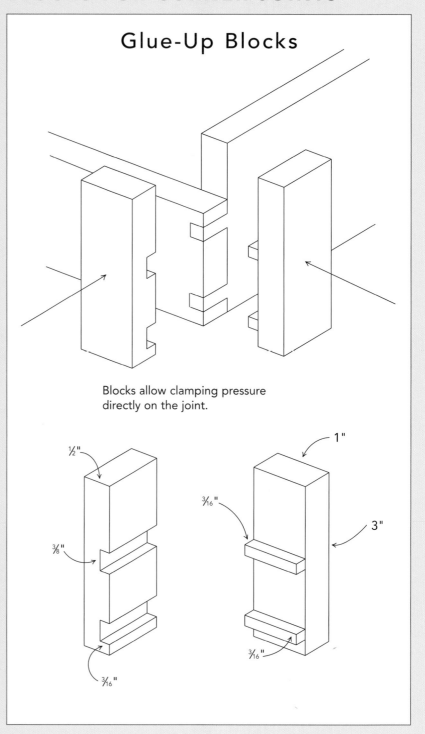

Glue-Up Blocks

Blocks allow clamping pressure directly on the joint.

½"

⅜"

³⁄₁₆"

1"

³⁄₁₆"

3"

³⁄₁₆"

PHOTO F: Clamp up the tray using blocks that put pressure only on the parts of the joint that need it.

Glue-Up

1. Cut the bottom so that it fits comfortably in the grooves between the sides. It should be large enough that it doesn't move around but not so large that it interferes with closing the joints. This is a plywood bottom so wood movement will not be a problem.

2. Finish-sand both sides of the bottom and the insides of the tray sides to 150 grit, and dry-fit all the parts just to make sure everything goes together easily. You don't want to have any surprises during actual glue-up.

3. Make glue blocks for clamping that put pressure only on the parts of the joints that need it (see "Custom Glue Blocks for Corner Joints").

4. Disassemble the tray, and apply glue to all mating surfaces. Leave a small amount of glue in the corners of the grooves for the bottom, so that it will help reinforce the tray

corners. Be as neat as possible when applying the glue; the less squeeze-out you have on the inside of the tray the better. It's difficult to do a good job of cleaning glue out of the corners of a finished piece.

5. Carefully assemble and clamp the piece, making sure that it remains square while clamping (see **photo F**).

Finishing

When the glue is dry, remove the clamps, finish-sand the outside of the tray to 150 grit, and finish your tray. Don't forget to sand the insides of the handle openings. I finished my tray with satin spray lacquer for durability. If you don't have the ability to spray, then you can certainly use an oil finish. I suggest a polymerized tung oil since it is the most durable of the oil finishes I have used.

DESIGN OPTION: SLIM-PROFILE TRAY

I chose to build this tray with the handle openings higher than the sides, partly for looks but also because I think it is a little easier to get your fingers into the higher openings when the tray is full.

The one down side to this design is that it is a little harder to store with the handles sticking up. If you feel this might be a problem, you can build a variation with lower sides. The construction is virtually the same, possibly a smidgen easier.

You will not need to perform step 7 in the short-side sequence (see p. 84). However, you will have to change the size of the template for routing the handle openings. The height of the opening will also have to be reduced from 1 in. to ¾ in. to fit in the same space.

Alternatively, you could make the sides higher all around if you would like to retain the larger handle opening.

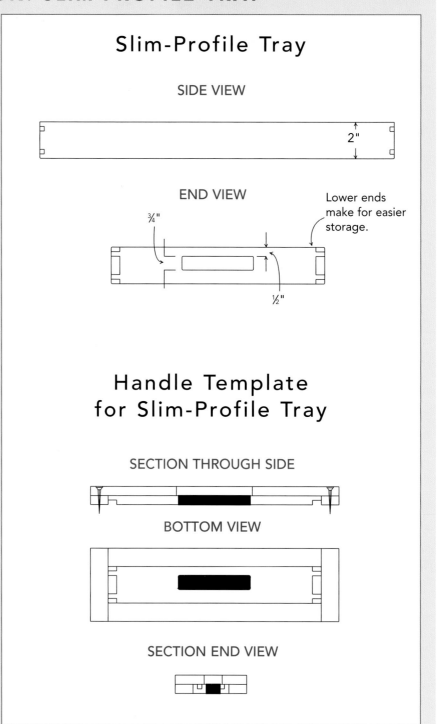

Slim-Profile Tray

SIDE VIEW

2"

END VIEW

¾"

Lower ends make for easier storage.

½"

Handle Template for Slim-Profile Tray

SECTION THROUGH SIDE

BOTTOM VIEW

SECTION END VIEW

LAZY SUSAN

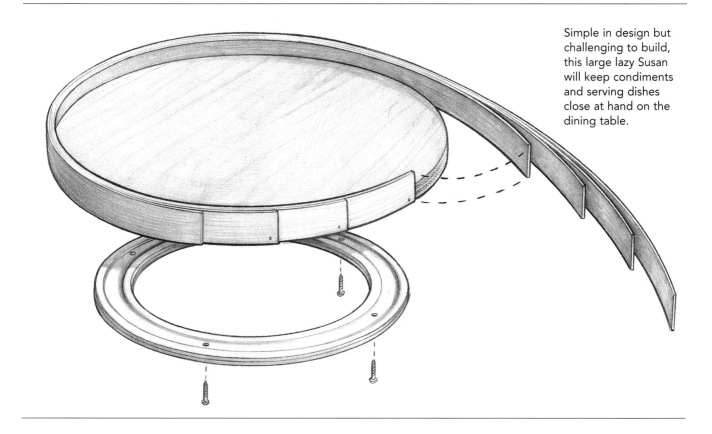

Simple in design but challenging to build, this large lazy Susan will keep condiments and serving dishes close at hand on the dining table.

CUT LIST FOR LAZY SUSAN

1	Circular base	24" x 24" x ¾"	mahogany plywood
5	Edge laminating strips	1¾" x ³⁄₃₂" x 66"	solid mahogany

Other materials
Epoxy
16" dia. turntable with screws

Construction and Assembly

I BUILT THIS LAZY SUSAN in mahogany to match the tray in this chapter. I also had some ¾-in.-thick mahogany plywood left over from the wine rack. As with the tray, you could use some other wood more to your liking. I would caution against the more open-grained, splintery wood, such as oak, since it would be more likely to split during the laminating process.

Since you have gotten this far, I'll assume I didn't scare you away with my rather cryptic warning about this project in the introduction to this chapter. I was referring to the laminated edge around the base of the lazy Susan, and it is really not too bad.

Top and Side Views

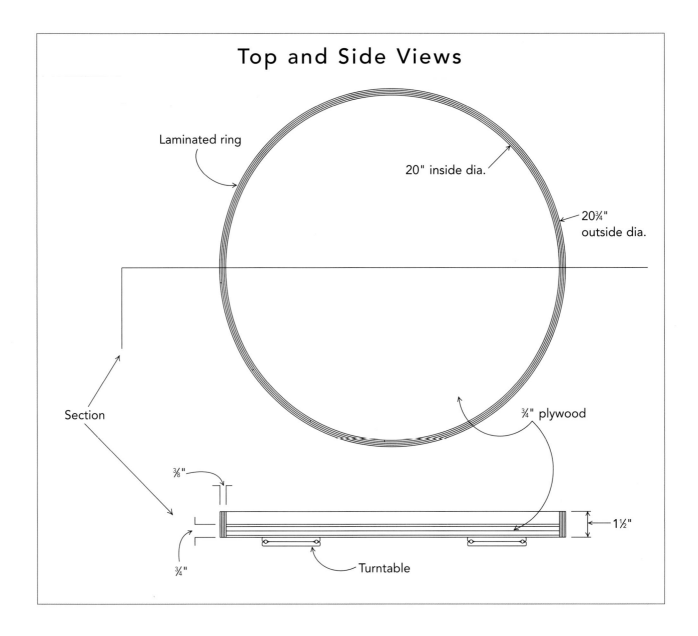

Laminated ring

20" inside dia.

20¾" outside dia.

Section

¾" plywood

⅜"

1½"

¾"

Turntable

This laminating technique is a valuable one to have in your repertoire, so whatever happens it will be time well spent. Also, the parts for this project are easily and quickly made, so it won't take any time to make extras if things don't work out the first time. Having said all that, if you follow along closely with me, and make sure you have some help during the laminating stage, all will be well.

This is a good time to point out that this is a very large lazy Susan. You can certainly build one smaller; however, bear in mind that a circle much smaller than this one may require thinner strips of wood to bend around and build the edge.

Forming the Circular Base

You start with two plywood circles, exactly the same size. One is for the base of the lazy Susan and one supports the edge during glue-up. The laminated edge is ¾ in. higher than the surface of the lazy Susan so it will need to be backed up during the laminating

PHOTO G: Shape the plywood circles on the lathe, roughing the shape with a gouge and truing the edge with a skew.

process. I find the quickest and easiest way to make the circles is on the lathe. However, if your lathe doesn't have this capacity or you don't have a lathe, then the next best method is to use a trammel with your router.

1. Get a piece of scrap plywood approximately 2 ft. square to use for your template circle.

2. Mark the diagonals on both sides to get the center points.

3. Using a large compass or trammel points, draw a 20-in.-dia. circle on both sides. It is always useful to have this drawn on both sides as a reference, and it is easier to do now than later.

4. With a bandsaw or jigsaw, roughly cut out the circle leaving at least ⅛ in. all around.

5. Screw this to a faceplate, and mount the assembly on your lathe. From there, it is a simple matter of turning it to 20 in. dia.

6. Start with a large gouge and work at the edge to get things close (see **photo G**). Then

switch to a skew and true the edge. It's important that the edge is square or it will not correctly support the laminated edge of the lazy Susan during the laminating process. Also, it's important for the edge to be square because you will be using this circle as a template to make the finished piece for the base.

7. Cover the edge and a little of the underside of the template circle with some wide packing tape. This will keep this piece from sticking to the finished lazy Susan when you glue on the edge.

8. Mark and rough out a circle of the same dimensions in mahogany plywood for the base.

9. Using double-sided tape, stick the template to the roughed-out mahogany piece.

The reason you place the tape on the template first is that it changes the diameter of the template, and it is important that both circles be exactly the same size. If you put the tape on later, after you size the strips

PHOTO H: Rout the lazy-Susan surface with a flush-trimming bit, using the template as a guide. Use double-sided tape instead of clamps to secure the work, so that you don't have to stop the cut halfway around.

for the edge, they will be too short. (This is one of those mistakes I alluded to in the introduction.)

10. Install a flush-trimming bit in your router.

11. Using the turned circle as a template, rout the mahogany piece to the same dimensions as the template (see **photo H**).

When I am routing around the entire edge of anything, I try to block up the workpiece so that I have access to all sides; that way, I can rout without stopping to reposition the workpiece. In this case I have attached a small plywood box to the underside of the assembly and to my worktable.

Laminating the Rim

Now comes the fun part! Along with the parts you already have, you will need two band clamps, a very sharp pencil or marking knife, some slow-set epoxy, a nice clear space, and a table saw with its miter gauge set for 90 degrees. Oh yes, and the assistance of some friendly, easygoing person for about an hour or so. (One more mistake I've made in the past!)

1. Rip and plane five strips of mahogany 1¼ in. wide by ³⁄₃₂ in. thick by 66 in. long. Four of these will make up the edge, and the fifth strip will be used as a clamping caul on the outside of all the other strips. (Yet another mistake I've made!)

2. Cut the ends of each piece square.

3. Separate the template and base circles, and finish-sand the top of the mahogany circle to 150 grit.

4. Lay both circles on top of each other, with the mahogany base on the bottom.

5. Place a piece of ⅛-in. plywood, or something of approximately the same thickness, under the circles. (Still another mistake!) This will allow the edging to extend past the bottom of the lazy Susan, giving it some room in case some or all of the strips slide a little. You can sand this flush later, but you can't sand the plywood flush to the edging!

WHY USE EPOXY?

You may be wondering why I used epoxy for this project. Adhesives for this kind of work need several properties:

- **Long open time.** Spreading adhesive on the strips, and coordinating them and the clamps around the template and base, takes time.

- **Gap filling.** In any bent lamination, it is virtually impossible to completely close every gap between every piece. I feel this is important, even if it's just for cosmetic reasons.

- **Waterproofing ability**. This is not absolutely essential, but I feel if you are going to this much trouble, you might as well protect the piece from moisture while you are at it.

There are three adhesive choices, in my opinion, that meet these criteria: modified urea-formaldehyde adhesive, epoxy, and polyurethane.

I usually reserve polyurethane for more light-duty applications, where the joints aren't under much stress. Though it's not supposed to creep, it does remain flexible, which makes me worry about leaving it under stress long term.

Either of the two remaining adhesives work fine for bent laminating. Of these two, however, epoxy has one really useful property for this particular application: It's slippery! In a circle lamination, you are forcing the faces of the laminates together as you tighten the band clamps around the strips. The harder you clamp, the harder it is for the strips to slide past one another. Modified urea formaldehyde doesn't reduce the friction between the parts as well as epoxy. It will have a tendency to grab, making it virtually impossible to completely close the circle. (Please don't ask me how I know this!)

---

6. With the aid of your assistant, wrap the first strip around the circles, overlapping the ends. Wrap a band clamp around the strip and tighten it as tightly as possible; mark where the ends overlap (see **photo I** on p. 94).

7. Take this apart. Using your table saw and miter gauge, trim the strip, splitting your mark. This should actually leave the strip a tiny bit long. While you can trim off some more, you can't put it back. (Did I mention I made a few errors along the way?)

8. Place the strip back on the circles with the band clamp tight. Check the fit and adjust if necessary. The ends of the strip should just meet when the band clamp is tight.

9. Repeat this procedure four more times, adding each new strip over the previous

strip. (That helper is really coming in handy now!) (See "Rim Detail" on p. 95 for spacing the ends of the strips.)

10. Make sure to number the strips somewhere where it won't show. You don't want to be trying to figure out which is which during glue-up.

11. Take the fifth strip and cover the inside face with some packing tape. This one is your clamping caul—you don't want it sticking to the others.

12. Lay out the second, third, and fourth strips inside face up.

13. Mix up some epoxy and spread it on these faces. Also spread epoxy on the edge of the mahogany circle. Try to keep the upper ⅛ in. of the edge clean of epoxy, so you will have as little squeeze-out on the inside of the lazy Susan as possible.

PHOTO I: Clamp up each edge strip around the template and base circles, marking where the ends overlap.

14. Stack all the strips together, in order, with the end of each strip offset from the one before it by about 4 in. to 5 in. This way the joints won't end up laying one over the other.

15. Together with your helper, wrap this assembly around the circles, folding the ends together as you go. Place one band clamp around everything, and tighten it until it is loosely holding things in place.

16. Push in down to the bottom of the edge, and place another band clamp above it.

17. Alternating from one clamp to the other, tighten them bit by bit until they are both as tight as they can possibly be.

Now that you have finished, I'll tell you that you have just completed the most difficult of all bent-laminate processes: "the complete circle." I didn't want to tell you earlier, in case you would totally freak out. Now go to bed! It will all look better in the morning.

Finishing

When the epoxy has cured (usually overnight), remove the clamps and clamping caul, and inspect your work. I'm sure it looks lovely.

1. Sand the bottom edge of the rim flush with the bottom of the base.

Rim Detail

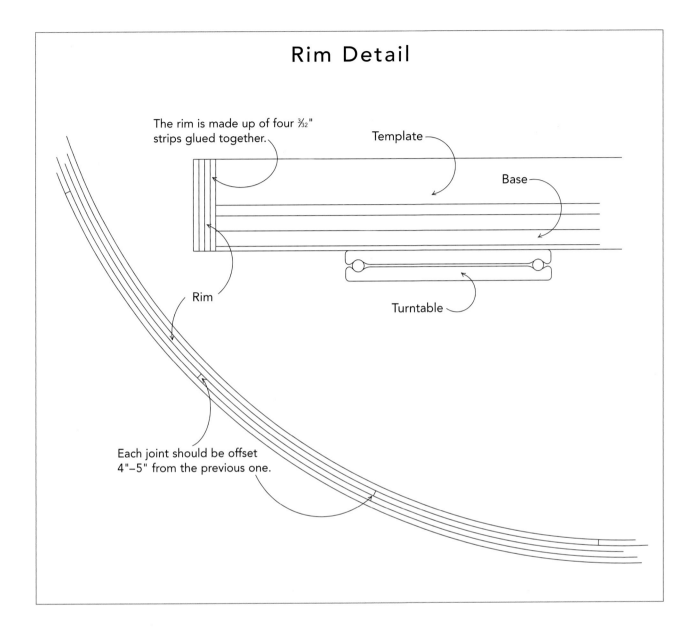

The rim is made up of four ³⁄₃₂" strips glued together.

Template

Base

Rim

Turntable

Each joint should be offset 4"–5" from the previous one.

2. Clamp a piece of plywood about 9 in. to 10 in. high to your table-saw fence, and lock the fence down 1½ in. from the blade.

3. Lower the blade to about ½ in. above the table, and saw off the excess height of the rim. Keep the bottom of the lazy Susan firmly against the plywood fence, and slowly rotate it past the blade.

4. When this is done, finish-sand the piece to 150 grit and apply a finish.

As with the tray, I finished my lazy Susan with satin spray lacquer for durability. You could also use an oil finish. I suggest a polymerized tung oil, again for its durability.

5. Attach the turntable. Exact instructions will come with the particular turntable you purchase, but it is usually just a matter of attaching a few screws.

HANGING POT RACK

POTS AND PANS PRESENT ONE of the more difficult and frustrating storage problems in the kitchen. Since they are often the largest kitchen utensils, even a small set can take up a considerable amount of space. We often end up stacking pans one inside the other in an effort to save space. This can lead to scratched and damaged pots. And inevitably, the one we need is always on the bottom. The most common place that pots and pans end up is inside a base cabinet. In this location, finding the right pot often requires crawling, or at least kneeling, on the floor.

Commercial kitchens solve these problems by hanging pots and pans overhead on racks designed for this purpose. Usually made from metal and quite large, these racks can be ungainly. They can look out of place it some kitchens. Also, it can be difficult to safely hang these racks from a residential ceiling,

since they can be quite heavy by themselves, before ever adding a pot!

The rack presented here is an elegant and practical solution to storing your cookware. It has the warmth of wood construction, and it is sized to fit the scale of a normal kitchen. In a kitchen with an average ceiling height (approximately 8 ft.), a pot rack should hang 16 in. down from the ceiling. This would put the top of the rack at 80 in. off the floor, about the height of the average doorway. This can, of course, be varied according to personal taste. Just remember that they shouldn't be hung so high that you need a stool to reach everything or so low that the pots hang in your way. Often, they are hung over an island so they are centrally located and close to the action but away from the worst of the cooking grease and out of forehead-striking distance.

HANGING POT RACK

This wood rack can give any kitchen the convenience of professional pot storage. Blocks with hooks ride in channels formed by rabbets in the crosspieces. The frame is attached to the ceiling with metal chains.

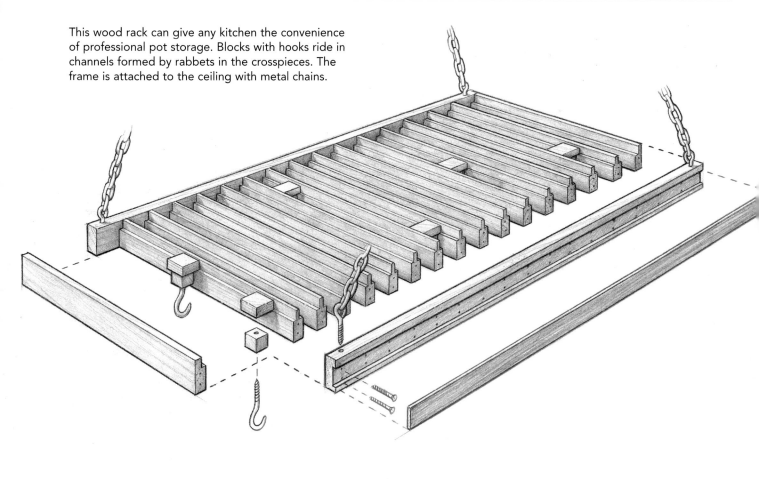

Construction and Assembly

THE RACK IS EASY TO MAKE. The pots hang from hooks set into blocks, which rest on the top edge of the rabbets in the crosspieces. The one trick, however, is that the crosspieces must be evenly spaced so that the hook plates ride freely on them but don't fall through. You want to be able to fit the hooks into any space.

Dimensioning the Parts

1. Mill the rails, stiles, and crosspieces from solid butternut to the dimensions in the cut list.

2. To mill the strips that cover the screw holes, you can either plane down thicker stock, or resaw a 4/4 board on the bandsaw then plane it to thickness. Mill the stock slightly larger in all three dimensions, so you can fit the pieces to their respective grooves.

3. Mill stock for the hook blocks. To make six blocks, you'll need either 6/4 lumber or two layers of ⅝-in.-thick stock, glued face to face. The 1¼-in.-thick blank should be 10 in. long by 1⅜ in. wide.

Side, Top, and End Views

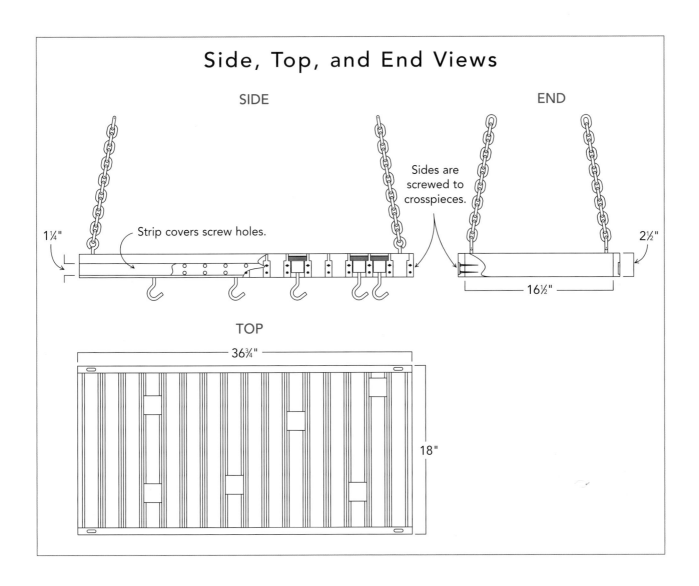

SIDE

END

1¼"

Strip covers screw holes.

Sides are screwed to crosspieces.

2½"

16½"

TOP

36¾"

18"

CUT LIST FOR HANGING POT RACK		
15 Crosspieces	16½" x 2½" x ¾"	solid butternut
2 Rails	16½" x 2½" x ¾"	solid butternut
2 Stiles	36¾" x 2½" x ¾"	solid butternut
2 Strips to cover screws	36¾" x 1¼" x 3⁄16"	solid butternut
6 Hook block	1⅜" x 1⅜" x 1¼"	solid butternut
6 Hook plate	2" x 2" x ½"	Baltic birch plywood
Other materials		
92 Wood screws	#8 x 1½"	
6+ Chrome hooks	4⅞" x 5⁄16"	
4 Eyebolts	sized for the chain	
Chain, as necessary		

4. For the hook plates, cut 2-in. squares of ½-in.-thick plywood. I used Baltic birch, but since the plates don't show, it doesn't much matter what type of plywood you use.

Machining and Assembly

The joinery is very straightforward; the crosspieces are simply screwed to the frame. The whole assembly is stronger than it needs to be because of all the parts. The only substantial work is in cutting the rabbets on the tops of the crosspieces, which I did on the router table.

1. Fit a ¾-in.-wide straight bit, at least 1 in. long, in your router table.

2. Set the height of the bit to ¾ in.

3. Taking multiple passes, cut the rabbet ¼ in. deep on both sides of the top edge of the crosspieces and on the inside top edge of the rails of the frame (see **photo A**).

4. Make 32 spacers, 1½ in. wide by 2½ in. tall, from scrap plywood or solid wood. Make them as close to 1½ in. wide as possible. Small variations in width will be multiplied 32 times.

5. Trial-fit the frame and crosspieces together, fitting the spacers between each crosspiece to keep their spacing consistent. It's a bit of a juggling trick with all the pieces and clamps involved.

6. Adjust the width of the spacers, if necessary, to ensure that the rails meet the stiles and all of the crosspieces are equally spaced.

7. Finish-sand all the pieces to 150 grit.

8. Apply a small line of glue on the end of each rail, keeping it away from the inside edge, and clamp up the entire assembly with

Hook Block Detail

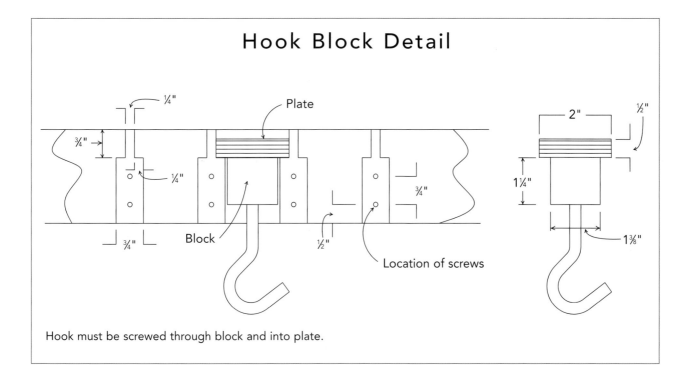

Plate

¼"

¾"

¼"

¾"

Block

½"

Location of screws

¾"

2"

½"

1¼"

1⅜"

Hook must be screwed through block and into plate.

the spacers in place. You need to avoid glue squeeze-out to ensure that you don't glue the spacers in place. The crosspieces don't need glue.

9. Drill pilot holes for screws through the stiles, centered on the crosspieces and rails (for screw location, see "Hook Block Detail"). Countersink the holes deeply, so that the screw heads sit at least ¼ in. below the surface of the stiles (see **photo B**).

Covering the Screw Holes

To cover the screw heads, you'll need to rout a groove on the stiles and fit strips to cover the holes.

1. Lower the ¾-in.-wide straight bit in the router table to cut 3⁄16 in. deep.

2. Check that no screw heads are shallower than ¼ in. You don't want to hit a screw with the router bit.

3. In two overlapping passes, cut a 1¼-in.-wide groove across the screw holes on the stiles (see **photo C** on p. 102).

PHOTO B: Screw the crosspieces to the stiles using spacer blocks between each to align them. Countersink the holes so that the heads sit at least ¼ in. below the face of the stile.

PHOTO C: Cut a wide groove on the faces of the stiles with overlapping cuts on the router table. Be sure to cut over both rows of screw heads.

PHOTO D: Make and fit solid-wood strips to fill the grooves. They effectively hide the screws joining the piece.

4. Fit the strips you milled earlier into the grooves, by trimming them to width. Leave the thickness and length oversize for now.
5. Glue and clamp the strips in place (see **photo D**).
6. When the glue has set, sand the strips flush with the stiles, and trim the ends flush with the rails.

Assembling the Hook Blocks

You need to make blocks and plates that fit and slide freely between the crosspieces but that are wide enough to be secure (see "Hook Block Detail" on p. 101).
1. Lay out an X from corner to corner on the underside of the plywood hook plates. You'll use these to center the blocks on the plates.

2. Apply a light film of glue to the blocks, and clamp them to the plates.

3. When the glue dries, drill pilot holes, sized to the hooks in the blocks, all the way through both pieces.

4. Finish-sand the blocks to 150 grit.

5. Screw the hooks into the blocks and plates so that the threads capture both pieces. You really want the hook hanging from the plate rather than the block.

Finishing and Hanging

1. Apply an oil finish to the frame, crosspieces, and blocks. You can also choose not to finish this piece at all. The butternut will age beautifully on its own.

2. Size four pieces of chain to whatever length will make the frame hang at the height you need it.

3. Drill pilot holes for and attach eyebolts to the top four corners of the frame. You may need to open the eyebolt in a vise to capture the chain.

4. Set hooks in the ceiling above where you wish to hang the rack. Where and how you set the hooks depends on what type of ceiling you have and what's behind it. You must find something solid to connect to, because the frame and several pots and pans add up to a lot of weight. If you're uncomfortable finding a solid attachment in your ceiling, hire a professional to set the hooks for you.

5. Put the hook blocks into the frame from above (see **photo E**).

6. Hang the frame from the ceiling with the help of a friend or two.

SPICE DRAWER/SHELF

THIS PROJECT WAS INSPIRED by the rows of small drawers I have seen in many European kitchens, usually placed under a wall cabinet adjacent to the stove. They are called spice drawers because at one time they were indeed used to store loose spices. These days, they are more often used to store other items, but the name hangs on. Although these drawers are useful enough by themselves, I chose to add a shelf to make it a little more practical and to give more options for placement in the kitchen. It is just the right size to either hold its own on a large piece of wall or be slipped between a couple of cabinets.

This is one of those pieces that cries out for small-scale, visible joinery as well as thinner than usual materials. I chose ¼-in. finger joints (sometimes called box joints), which I think fit the scale of this piece perfectly. Repetitive joinery, such as finger joints, is a product of the machine age and was often used for packing and shipping containers and crates. These joints would be difficult to cut by hand, mostly because of the sheer number and (usually) diminutive size of the joints. They are, however, easily cut on the table saw with a simple jig. The setup is a little fussy and usually requires making a number of test pieces, but after that, you can cut these joints all day long!

SPICE DRAWER/SHELF

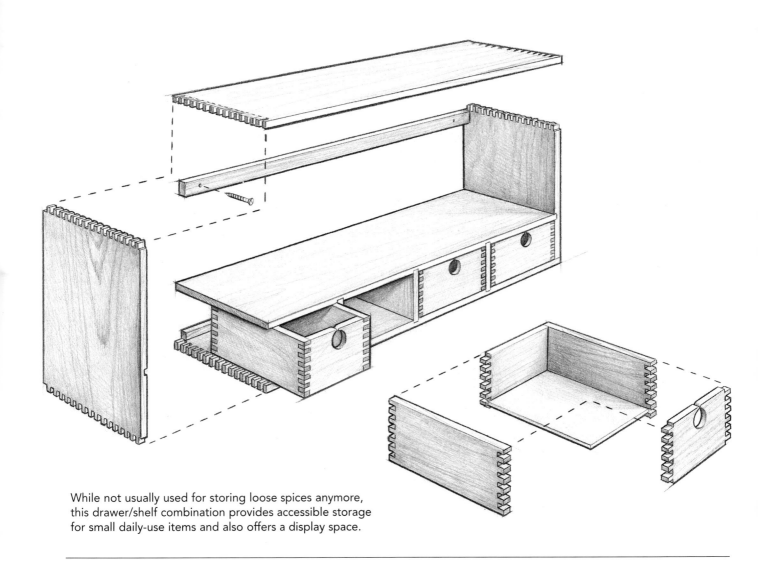

While not usually used for storing loose spices anymore, this drawer/shelf combination provides accessible storage for small daily-use items and also offers a display space.

Construction and Assembly

I CHOSE CHERRY FOR THIS PIECE, but you could certainly use another wood. I would, however, try to stay away from the more splintery wood, such as oak or ash, since the tiny joints might tend to break out.

Milling Parts

1. Mill the top and sides of the case and the front, back, and sides of the drawers to the dimensions in the cut list. These parts will all have finger joints. To mill stock this thin, you have several options, including planing down thicker stock or resawing (see "Thin Stock Options" on p. 57).

2. Mill several extra 8-in.-wide pieces for testing the finger joints.

Top, Front, and Side Views

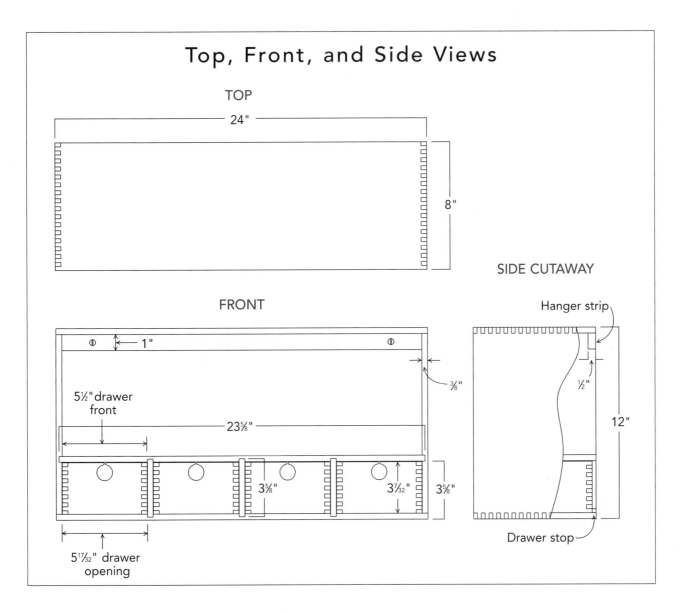

TOP

24"

8"

FRONT

1"

5½" drawer front

23⅝"

⅜"

3⅜"

3⁷⁄₃₂"

3⅝"

5¹⁷⁄₃₂" drawer opening

SIDE CUTAWAY

Hanger strip

½"

12"

Drawer stop

CUT LIST FOR SPICE DRAWER/SHELF		
2 Top and bottom	24" x 8" x ⅜"	solid cherry
1 Shelf	23⅝" x 8" x ⅜"	solid cherry
2 Sides	12" x 8" x ⅜"	solid cherry
3 Drawer dividers	3⅝" x 8" x ⅜"	solid cherry
1 Hanger strip	23¼" x 1" x ½"	solid cherry
8 Drawer sides	3¼" x 7¾" x ⅜"	solid cherry
8 Drawer fronts and backs	3¼" x 5½" x ⅜"	solid cherry
4 Drawer bottoms	5⅛" x 7⅜" x ¼"	solid cherry
4 Drawer stops	5¹⁷⁄₃₂" x ¼" x ¼"	solid cherry

3. Mill the shelf, dividers, drawer bottoms, hanger strip, and stock for the drawer stops to dimension. Leave the drawer-stop stock long for the moment. You'll fit it later to the actual openings.

Dadoing for the Dividers and Shelf

The shelf fits into dadoes in the case sides, and the drawer dividers fit into dadoes in the bottom of the shelf and the top of the bottom of the case. You want four evenly spaced drawer openings in the completed case.

1. The dadoes for the shelf are located $3\frac{5}{8}$ in. up from the bottom edge of the piece.

2. On the bottom of the case, the two outside dadoes for the drawer dividers are located $5\frac{29}{32}$ in. from the ends. The third dado is in the center.

3. On the shelf, the two outside dadoes are $5\frac{23}{32}$ in. from the ends of the board. The third dado is also centered.

4. Cut the dadoes on the table saw, using a $\frac{3}{8}$-in.-wide dado blade, set to cut $\frac{3}{16}$ in. deep.

Use the rip fence to locate the cut and the miter gauge to guide the piece in the cut. (See the spice and tea shelf, pp. 50–59, for detailed information on dadoing.)

Cutting the Finger Joints

The drawers and case sides are held together with finger joints. To cut consistently sized fingers, you'll first need to make a jig (see "Finger-Jointing Jig").

Joining the drawers

I cut the drawers so that the fronts and backs have end-grain pins showing at the top and bottom.

1. Cut the front and back pieces first. Make the first cut by placing a $\frac{1}{4}$-in. by $\frac{1}{4}$-in. spacer between the workpiece and the pin. (The leftover pin stock for the jig works well for this.) This makes the first cut at the very edge of the board (see **photo A**), so that the front and sides join with their edges flush.

PHOTO A: With a finger-jointing jig on the table saw, cut the fingers on the fronts and backs, making the first cut using a spacer block the thickness of the fingers.

PHOTO B: Make subsequent cuts in the fronts and backs, always positioning the registration pin in previous kerf.

FINGER-JOINTING JIG

A simple plywood auxiliary fence attached to the miter gauge makes an excellent jig for cutting finger joints. It should not take you more than a few minutes to make, and it's the only reasonable way to cut the joints.

1. Clamp an auxiliary plywood fence to your table saw's miter gauge, with several inches stretching across the line of cut.

2. Install a ¼-in.-wide dado cutter in your table saw, and raise it to cut a ⅜-in.-deep cut.

3. Run the auxiliary fence over the dado blade, cutting a notch in the bottom edge.

4. Mill a foot length of ¼-in. by ¼-in. pin stock.

5. Remove the auxiliary fence and glue in a 1½-in. length of the pin stock in the slot, flush with the back and bottom edge of the auxiliary fence. The workpiece will register against this pin. Put the rest of the pin stock to one side for the moment.

6. Reattach the auxiliary fence to the miter-gauge head so that the dado blade will cut a notch exactly ¼ in. to the left of the pin.

7. Cut two test pieces to ensure the jig works properly and cuts ¼-in. slots spaced exactly ¼ in. apart. The test pieces should slide together easily, with light hand pressure.

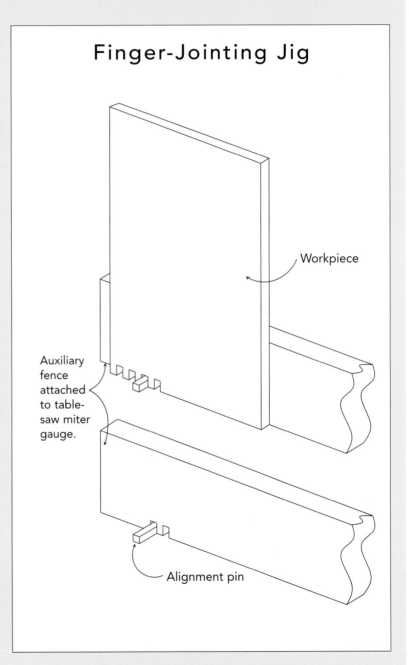

Finger-Jointing Jig

Workpiece

Auxiliary fence attached to table-saw miter gauge.

Alignment pin

2. Remove the spacer, lift the workpiece up, position the slot you just cut on the pin, and make the next cut.

3. The subsequent cuts follow the same pattern, moving the workpiece from left to right (see **photo B**).

4. For the pins in the side pieces, place the workpiece against the registration pin (without the spacer), and cut the first slot (see **photo C**).

5. All the subsequent cuts are the same as for the front and back.

Joining the case

1. Cut the joints in the top and bottom of the case, following the same technique used for cutting the sides of the drawers.

2. Cut the joints in the sides of the case, following the same technique used for cutting the fronts and backs of the drawers, using the spacer for the first cut.

PHOTO C: To cut the sides that mate with the fronts and backs, make the first cut with the side of the workpiece (without the spacer) butting against the registration pin. This will start a complementary pattern of kerfs and fingers.

Grooving for the Drawer Bottoms

In the sides of the drawers, the groove will line up with the first notch. In the fronts, the groove will line up precisely with the first pin, removing half of the pin and leaving a void that you'll fill in a later step.

1. Set the rip fence on your table saw ¼ in. from the dado blade. Set the blade to cut ³⁄₁₆ in. deep.

2. Cut a ¼-in.-wide by ³⁄₁₆-in.-deep groove in the bottom inside edge of all drawer parts (see **photo D**).

3. Cut drawer bottoms to fit these grooves.

PHOTO D: Locate the groove for the drawer along the bottom edge of the drawer sides, aligned with the second finger/kerf pair.

Making the Drawer Pulls

1. Drill a 1-in.-dia. hole in the drawer fronts, centered ⅝ in. down from the top edge. Use a Forstner bit on a drill press, with a piece of scrap backing up the workpiece, so that the wood doesn't break out on the bottom side.

2. Using a small handsaw, cut a thin slot through the top edge of the drawer front into the hole (see "Making the Drawer Pull").

PHOTO E: Soften the edges of the handle detail with fine sandpaper, being careful not to reshape the kerf or file cuts.

3. File a slight V in the top and bottom of the kerf using a small triangular file.

4. Round all the edges slightly with sandpaper (see **photo E**).

Assembling the Drawers

1. Dry-fit all the drawers and adjust the fit as necessary, making sure the drawer bottom has at least 1/16 in. of room side to side, to allow for seasonal wood movement.

2. Finish-sand the drawer parts to 150 grit.

3. Make clamping cauls to put even pressure across the joints. Put packing tape on the inside faces of the cauls to keep them from adhering to the drawers.

4. Brush glue on all the joint faces of one drawer but not on the drawer bottom or grooves.

5. Assemble and clamp the drawer, checking and adjusting for square. Repeat the process for the other three drawers.

6. When the glue has set, make 1/4-in. by 3/16-in. pegs, and plug the holes in the sides left from cutting the drawer-bottom grooves (see **photo F**).

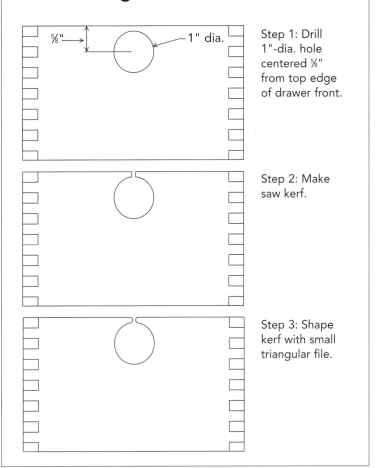

Making the Drawer Pull

5/8" 1" dia.

Step 1: Drill 1"-dia. hole centered 5/8" from top edge of drawer front.

Step 2: Make saw kerf.

Step 3: Shape kerf with small triangular file.

PHOTO F: After you assemble the drawers, fill the holes in the sides left from routing the drawer grooves.

PHOTO G: Assemble the case from the bottom up, fitting the drawer dividers, bottom, and shelf together first, then the sides, and lastly the top.

Drawer Details

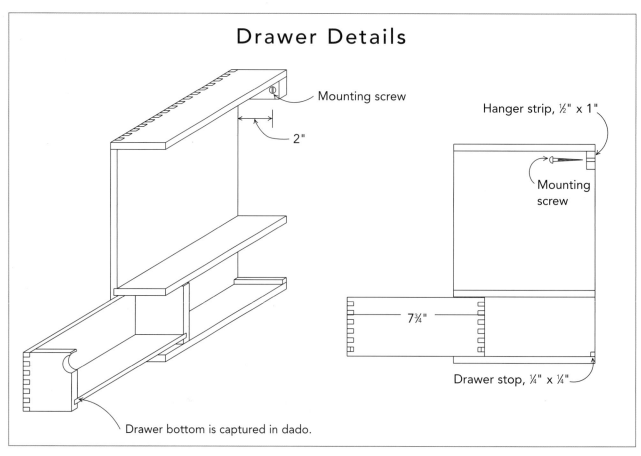

Mounting screw

2"

Hanger strip, ½" x 1"

Mounting screw

7¾"

Drawer stop, ¼" x ¼"

Drawer bottom is captured in dado.

Assembling and Finishing the Case

1. Glue and clamp the case together, starting with the bottom, drawer dividers, and shelf (see **photo G**). Next, glue and clamp the sides, followed by the top.

2. After the glue has set, remove the clamps and install a ¼-in. by ¼-in. drawer stop at the back of the case. These keep the fronts of the drawers flush with the front of the case.

Building them this way allows some front-to-back adjustment, if necessary, by changing the size of the stops.

3. Glue and clamp in place a ½-in. by 1-in. by 23¼-in. hanger strip in the inside top back edge of the piece. Be sure to drill holes for the screws you will be hanging it with before you glue it in place (see "Drawer Details").

4. Finish the case with oil and wax, or however you prefer.

DESIGN OPTION: DRAWERS ALONE

I designed this project to work well in any number of locations in your kitchen. However, the one location in which it would not work well is under an upper cabinet because the piece is rather tall. It's ironic since this is the traditional location of the small drawers that were the inspiration for this project.

However, if this style and location is more to your taste, then it is a simple matter to omit the shelf portion. You can also add or subtract drawers to better fit your chosen location.

To build this version, you'll simply need to put ¼-in. hanger strips behind the two outer drawers along the top inside edge of the case.

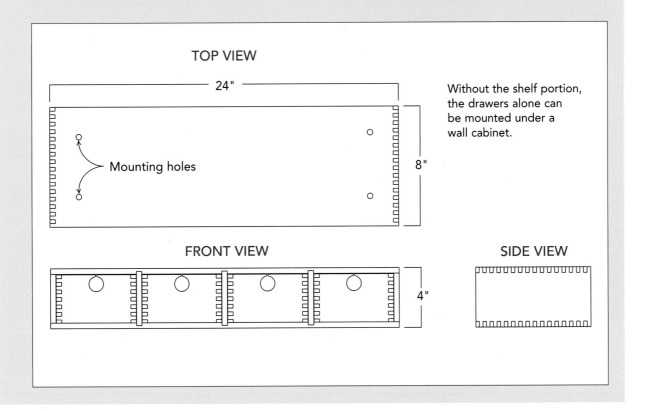

TOP VIEW

24"

Mounting holes

8"

Without the shelf portion, the drawers alone can be mounted under a wall cabinet.

FRONT VIEW

4"

SIDE VIEW

FOLDING STEP STOOL

THIS STEP STOOL SHOULD REALLY BE considered a storage project. Its entire purpose is to give you easy access to the top row of shelves in your kitchen—you know, the ones filled with seldom-used kitchen implements. But ask yourself: Are those implements seldom used because they're not very useful or because they're hard to reach? Certain types of kitchen chairs can be pressed into service, but generally they're awkward to get up on, and who likes to sit on their own footprints?

This folding step stool can be tucked in a low-traffic corner of the kitchen and put into service at a moment's notice. All that "dead" storage space up high suddenly becomes much more accessible and useful with a step stool around. My four-year-old son also likes having the stool in the kitchen. Unlike the adult-sized chairs, he can pick it up, move it, and get

on top easily—a perfect perch to watch his parents put dinner together.

The design is about as simple as it can be. The rear legs have a curve at the top that allows them to fold under. When opened, a corner on the top of the rear legs butts against the top step, locking the legs in place. The top step is centered over the base making it very sturdy. And it's still light enough to carry or push around with your foot.

FOLDING STEP STOOL

This sturdy step stool will give you 18" of added reach when standing on the top step. It folds compactly for easy storage.

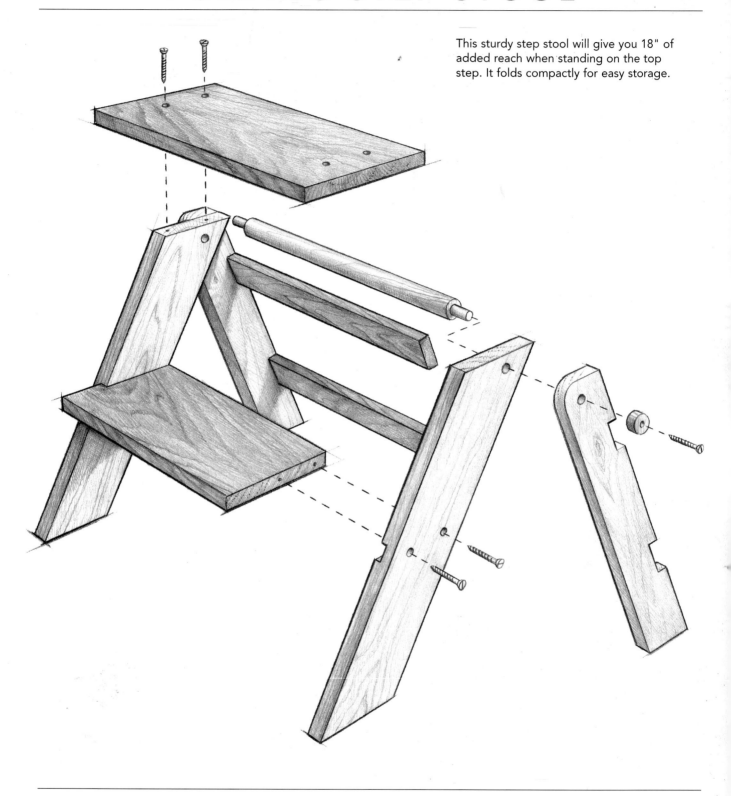

Views of Folding Step Stool

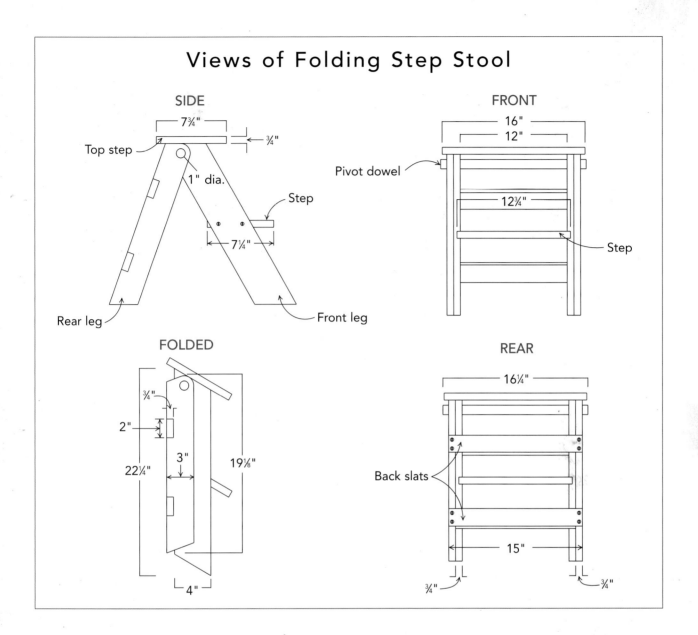

SIDE

7¾"

¾"

Top step

1" dia.

Step

7¼"

Rear leg

Front leg

FRONT

16"

12"

Pivot dowel

12¾"

Step

FOLDED

¾"

2"

22¼"

3"

19⅛"

4"

REAR

16¼"

Back slats

15"

¾"

¾"

Construction and Assembly

THE VERTICAL MEMBERS ARE in cherry, while the horizontal members are in walnut. I did this to add some visual interest. And dark walnut hides a bit better the dirt that all steps collect. There is no glue in this project. This means that precise connection of all the parts, especially the step into the legs, is crucial. The location of the pivot dowel on the legs is also crucial. Moving it even slightly will cause the stool's geometry to change. Use the dimensions

CUT LIST FOR STEP STOOL

1	Top step	16" x 7¾" x ¾"	solid walnut
1	Step	12¾" x 7¼" x ¾"	solid walnut
2	Front legs	22¼" x 4" x ¾"	solid cherry
2	Rear legs	19⁷⁄₁₆" x 3" x ¾"	solid cherry
2	Slats	15" x 2" x ¾"	solid walnut
1	Dowel blank	17½" x 1¼" x 1¼"	solid walnut

Other materials

12	Brass screws	#8 x 1¼"
4	Brass screws	#10 x 2"
2	Brass screws	#4 x 1"

Joinery Layout on Legs

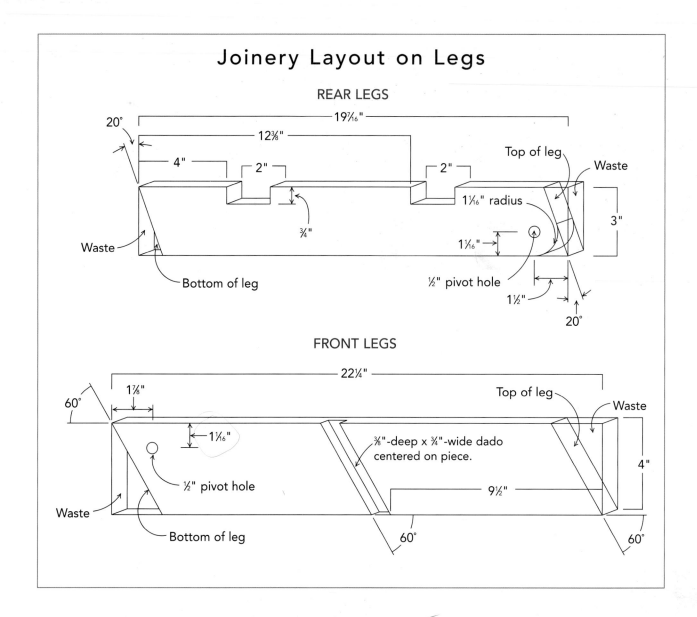

REAR LEGS

20°

19⁷/₁₆"

12⅜"

4"

2"

2"

Top of leg

Waste

1¹/₁₆" radius

3"

Waste

¾"

1¹/₁₆"

½" pivot hole

Bottom of leg

1½"

20°

FRONT LEGS

22¼"

60°

1⅞"

Top of leg

Waste

1¹/₁₆"

⅜"-deep x ¾"-wide dado centered on piece.

4"

½" pivot hole

Waste

9½"

Bottom of leg

60°

60°

60°

---

indicated so that the rear legs can fold under without binding and can also fold out and lock at the proper angle for the stool to stand properly.

Milling and Layout

1. Mill the steps and slats to the dimensions in the cut list. Be precise because small discrepancies will conspire and multiply against you, and accurately sized parts will greatly facilitate final assembly. At this point, these parts are done.

2. Mill the four leg blanks to the dimensions in the cut list.

3. Lay out the slat notches, top and bottom angles, pivot points, and top curves on the rear legs. (Their locations are indicated in "Joinery Layout on Legs"). Be particular in the location of your layout lines, especially for the pivot points.

4. Lay out the step dadoes, top and bottom angles, and pivot points on the front legs. Mark the legs for left and right at this point, so you don't make mistakes later.

PHOTO A: To cut the tops and bottoms of the legs, use the miter gauge set at the proper angle to guide the workpiece. A stop block will ensure consistent leg lengths.

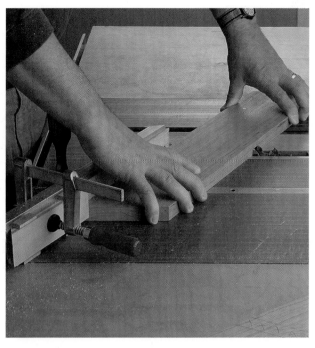

PHOTO B: With the miter gauge set at the same angle (60 degrees), cut the dadoes for the steps with a dado blade. Also use a stop block for consistent location.

Shaping the Legs

1. Cut the tops and bottoms of the rear-leg blanks at 20-degree angles (see **photo A**). Use your miter gauge to set the appropriate angles shown in the drawing. Use a stop block to ensure the legs are the same length, and be sure to cut parallel ends.

2. Reset the miter gauge to cut at 60 degrees, and cut the top and bottom of the front legs in the same way.

3. Change the blade in the table saw to a ¾-in.-wide dado blade. Set the blade to cut ⅜ in. deep.

4. Using the same angle setting on your miter gauge (60 degrees), cut the dadoes for the steps on the inside faces of the left and right front legs (see **photo B**).

5. Raise the dado blade to cut ¾ in. deep and reset your miter gauge to 90 degrees.

6. Cut notches in the rear legs for the slats (see **photo C**). The notches are 2 in. wide, so the dado blade isn't wide enough to cut

PHOTO C: Cut the notches for the slats in the rear legs with the dado blade at 90 degrees and the miter fence at 90 degrees.

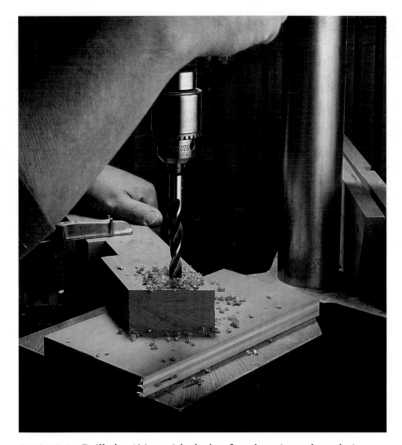

PHOTO D: Drill the ½-in.-wide holes for the pivot dowels in both the rear legs (shown) and the front legs on the drill press. Clamp each pair of legs together to ensure the holes line up.

them in one pass. Make several overlapping cuts, nibbling away at the waste, up to your layout lines.

7. Clamp the front legs together with the inside faces touching.

8. On a drill press, drill the ½-in. pivot holes through both legs at once, exactly on your layout mark. Do the same for the rear legs (see **photo D**).

9. Cut the curve at the top of the rear legs with a jigsaw or a bandsaw, and sand to the layout line. Cut slowly and as close to the line as you can, making sure the cut is square to the face of the leg. It is important that you get this curve right. If the curve is too large, it will bind against the top step when you fold the stool. If the curve is too small, the stool will not stand correctly when opened.

Turning the Pivot Dowel

The rear legs pivot on the dowel, allowing the stool to fold. The dowel fits into the holes drilled in the front and rear legs, and is locked in place between the front legs. The

PHOTO E: Turn the pivot areas on the dowels to exactly ½ in. dia., so that the dowel fits the holes in the leg snugly. For best results, check the diameter often as you turn.

Steps for Shaping Pivot Dowel

Step 1:
Start with square turning blank.

1¼"

1¼" →

17½"

Step 2:
Turn to 1" dia.

1" dia. —

Step 3:
Turn two 2"-long sections to exactly ½" dia.

2"

½"

1"

Step 4:
Saw off end pieces.

12"

¾"

Step 5:
Drill ½" hole in each end piece.

caps screwed into the ends are purely decorative (see "Steps for Shaping Pivot Dowel").
1. Turn the entire 1¼-in.-square dowel blank to 1 in. dia. The exact diameter is not important. Since turning reasonably perfect cylinders can be difficult, you might want to start with a hardwood dowel (see Resources on p. 165).

2. Lay out the pivot areas on both ends of the dowel, 12 in. apart and each 2 in. long. There should be ¾ in. left at either end.
3. Turn the pivot areas down to exactly ½ in. dia. (see **photo E**). The ends of the dowel have to fit precisely into the ½-in. holes you drilled in the legs.
4. Finish-sand the dowel on the lathe.

5. Take the blank off the lathe, and cut off the caps at the ends (see **photo F**).

6. Drill ½-in.-dia. holes ⁷⁄₁₆ in. deep in the caps, using the same drill bit you used to drill the holes in the legs (see **photo G**).

7. Finish-sand the cut ends of the caps.

PHOTO F: Cut the end caps off the turned dowel blank with a handsaw, and save them.

PHOTO G: Drill ½-in.-dia. holes centered in the faces of the end caps. Drill on the face that was chucked in the lathe to hide any chuck marks.

Preassembly and Fitting

1. Assemble and clamp together the front legs, step, and pivot dowel. The step should be tight in the dado, which will help keep the parts square. Align the step so that the top rear edge is flush with the back edge of the leg.

2. Mark the locations for the screws that will attach the step to the legs, 1 in. in from the sides of the legs and centered on the dado.

3. Drill pilot holes and countersink for #8 by 1¼-in. screws.

4. Screw the step to the legs using steel screws. In all cases, these steel screws will be replaced with decorative brass screws during final assembly (see "Using Brass Screws").

5. Place the front-leg assembly front down on the bench. It will rest awkwardly on the step, but that's all right.

6. Fit the rear legs onto the pivots, with the dadoes facing up.

7. Slide a playing card (or something of equal thickness, such as a business card) between each front and rear leg, one near the pivot and one near the step. Clamp the legs together, placing the clamps over the playing cards.

8. Fit the slats in their dadoes, making sure they're flush with the outside edge of the rear legs. If the slats are too short or too thin, adjust the thickness of your playing-card shims. You can also remove the shims from just one side.

9. Mark and drill two countersunk pilot holes on each end of the slats. Assemble the rear legs and slats with steel screws.

10. Test the action of the rear legs, making sure that the top curves don't extend beyond the top edges of the front legs at any point in their movement arc. If the curves are proud, sand them.

11. Drill and countersink four pilot holes on the top, 1⅜ in. from each side, 2 in. from the back edge, and 2¾ in. from the front

PHOTO H: Assemble the stool with the brass screws only after you've pre-assembled it with steel screws of the same size. This will help you avoid breaking off a brass screw.

edge. These pilot holes should intersect the tops of the front legs 1¾₆ in. from the back edge and ½ in. from the front edge. You don't want the 2-in.-long screws to break out of the legs.

12. Attach the top to the front legs with steel screws. Test the action of the folding stool, and see if it stands straight. Make any adjustments necessary.

13. Slide the caps onto the ends of the pivot dowels, and drill a countersunk pilot hole for the #4 by 1-in. screws in the center.

14. Disassemble the entire stool, and finish-sand to 150 grit. However, don't sand the ends of the step that fits into the dadoes. You don't want to remove more material and risk changing the fit.

Assembly and Finishing

Because you don't use glue in the construction, you can finish all the parts separately, which is much easier.

USING BRASS SCREWS

Brass screws add a touch of beauty where silver steel screws just don't. The problem with brass screws, as anyone who has ever used them knows, is that they break easily. Few tasks are as exasperating as extracting a broken screw. There's no easy way to remove it without tearing up the wood. Here are a few tips for preventing those enraging breaks.

• Start with high-quality brass screws. The cheaper hardware-store varieties are made from inferior alloys and break much more easily. I have found that the best brass screws are darker in color, a reddish gold rather than a yellowish gold.

• Compared to drilling pilot holes for steel wood screws, holes for brass screws should be a trifle wider but not so wide that the threads don't catch. They should drive in easily by hand. Power drills should be avoided. Very small brass screws should be driven in with finger pressure.

• A good strategy is to use steel screws of the same size for all pre-assembly work, especially when you have to drive and remove the screws repeatedly. When all is finished, you can remove the steel screws and carefully drive the brass screws in place once and only once.

• Use the correct-sized cabinetmaker's screwdriver, especially if it's a slot screw. The width of the screwdriver blade should be the same as the length of the slot. Smaller blades will cut into the soft brass and are more apt to cam out of the slot.

1. Apply an oil finish to all the parts. I would not use a film finish, such as a lacquer or varnish, for this project because the legs slide against one another. A film finish would get in the way and get scratched up to boot. Let the finish cure.

2. Put the stool back together again, using brass screws (see **photo H**).

COUNTRY PINE TABLE

EVERY WOODWORKER WHO HAS SPENT a whole afternoon trying to get miter joints to fit perfectly knows the meaning of frustration. And every one of those woodworkers, myself included, needs what I call a "woodworking vacation." This is a project in which errors do not detract from, but add to, the value.

I'm not talking about significant errors such as joints that don't fit, but those little errors such as sanding scratches, small chunks of short grain torn from a turned leg, and cracks. In certain projects, such as this country-style table, these types of errors help to make the table look older, well used, and part of the family. As a project, it's a joy to build because you can be fast and loose, and the mistakes do not add hours of frustrating work. In fact, making it perfect will lessen the table's appeal. How easy is this table to make? It should only take a leisurely weekend to complete.

Around where I live, there are a fair number of old farms. The barns get torn down from time to time, yielding a supply of old hemlock beams. I used a few to build this kitchen table; though new, it already looks 100 years old. If you can't find salvaged lumber, then knotty pine, spruce, or Douglas fir will work well. If turning the legs puts you off, you can find preturned legs through catalogs and from small businesses (see Resources on p. 165).

COUNTRY PINE TABLE

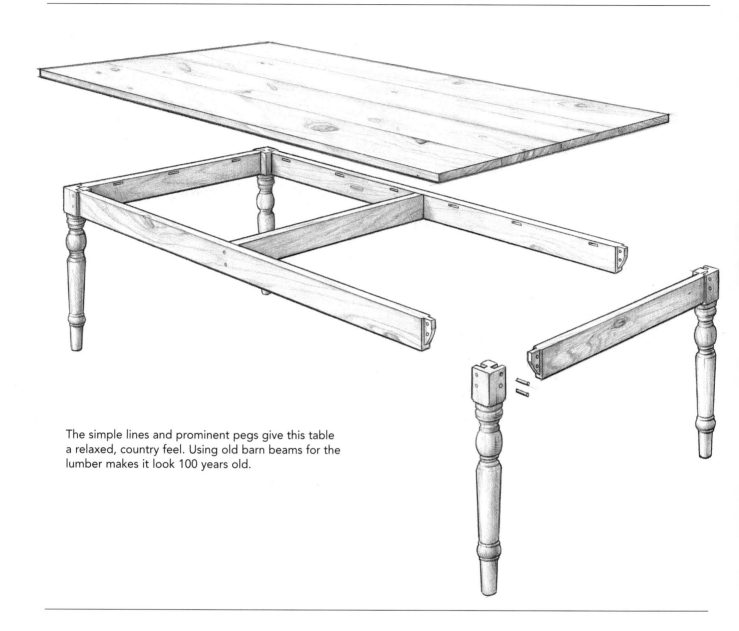

The simple lines and prominent pegs give this table a relaxed, country feel. Using old barn beams for the lumber makes it look 100 years old.

Construction and Assembly

NO PART OF THE construction is an exact science. The joints need to be tight, of course, but otherwise you can change and adapt measurements to suit the size of your kitchen. Keep in mind that you should have a good 3 ft. of space on all four sides of a table for access.

Milling and Assembling the Parts

1. Mill enough planks for the top to thickness. For a finished width of 36 in. and a length of 66 in., you should start with enough boards for a blank at least 38 in. wide and 68 in. long. It's easier to trim to size afterward, and you won't have to fuss with clamping blocks to avoid denting the edges.

Top, Side, and End Views

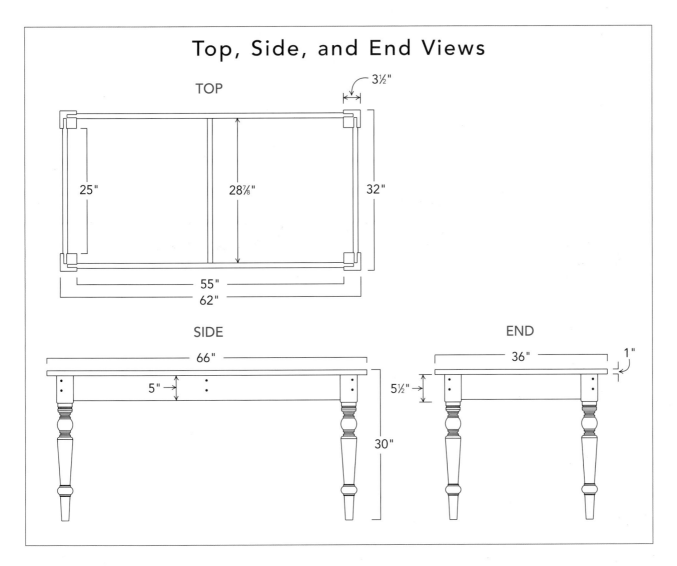

TOP

3½"

25"   28⅞"   32"

55"

62"

SIDE

66"

5" →

30"

END

36"

1"

5½" →

2. Edge-glue the boards for the top blank quickly and without worrying too much about alignment. Biscuits aren't necessary and are, in fact, counterproductive, because they will make boards align too well.

3. Once the glue is dry, trim the top to size. Crosscut the ends first (see **photo A** on p. 128), then rip the sides to width. To do this work, I used an aluminum guide rail with a circular saw. You might also be able to do this by rough cutting with a jigsaw, then cleaning up the edges with a straightedge and router.

4. Sand the top with rough sandpaper, such as 60 grit, to level all the joints. You're not trying to flatten the top but simply smooth the joints (see **photo B** on p. 128).

CUT LIST FOR COUNTRY PINE TABLE

4	Legs	29" x 3½" x ¾₁₂"	solid hemlock
2	Long aprons	59" x 5" x 1"	solid hemlock
2	Short aprons	29" x 5" x 1"	solid hemlock
1	Center support	28⅞" x 5" x 1"	solid hemlock
1	Top	66" x 36" x 1"	solid hemlock

Other materials

21	Tabletop fasteners
20	Dowel pins

PHOTO A: With a circular saw and guide, cut the ends of the top blank square to the sides. The top is too large to crosscut safely on a table saw without a sliding table.

PHOTO B: Sand the top to remove glue squeeze-out, but not to a polished finish. Leave gouges and scratches and some unevenness for a very old look.

5. Finish-sand, skipping grits to a maximum of 120, without removing all of the scratches from the coarser grits. The result will be a pleasantly uneven surface, with a patina of seeming wear and use—smooth without being shiny or glass-perfect.

6. Mill the leg blanks to size. If you don't have or can't get 4-in. by 4-in. blanks, then mill and glue up 8/4 boards to size.

7. Mill the aprons and the center support to the dimensions listed on the cut list. You should make the aprons a few inches longer than necessary and trim off the excess when you cut the tenons.

8. Finish-sand the aprons, again skipping grits, to a maximum of 120.

Turning the Legs

Though I've presented you with a pattern, feel free to turn any leg profile you like. If you're new to turning or don't have a lathe, you can always buy commercially turned legs.

Leg Profile

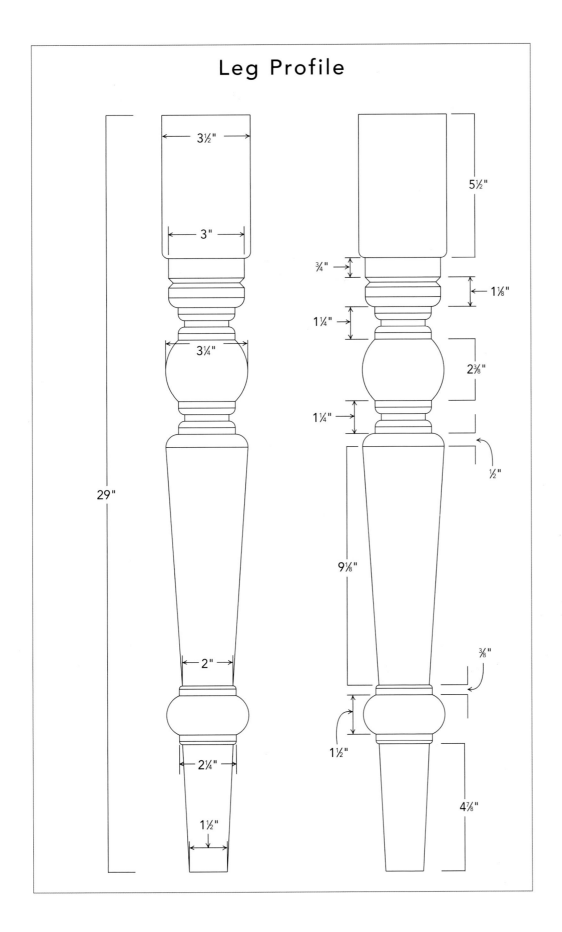

PHOTO C: After you make the registration cuts, start to shape the coves and beads with a spindle gouge.

PHOTO D: Use a skew to smooth the long, tapered sections in the leg.

1. Turn the square blanks to cylinders with a roughing-out gouge, leaving the top 5½ in. square.

2. Mark out the features on one leg, using the "Leg Profile" drawings as a guide (see p. 129).

3. Make registration cuts with a parting tool at each transition. Make these cuts to the finished diameters using calipers to measure.

4. Using whatever turning tools you're comfortable with, create the curves, shapes, and tapers between the registration cuts (see **photos C and D**). Consider mistakes as opportunities for design variations. For example, if you remove too much material where you wanted a ball, move the ball.

5. Transfer the locations of the turned features on your finished leg to the other leg blanks (see **photo E**). In keeping with the casual nature of this project, the legs need only be alike, not identical.

6. Turn the other three legs.

7. Sand each blank on the lathe to 100 grit.

Joinery

The joint used to connect the legs and aprons is an unconventional pegged mortise and tenon. It's straightforward to make, using a dado blade to cut both the mortise and the tenon (see "Leg and Apron Joint Detail").

Cutting the mortises and making the tenon template

You will be cutting two mortises at the top of each leg—one for the long apron and the other for the short apron.

1. Fit a ⅜-in.-wide dado blade into your table saw, and raise it to cut 2 in. deep.

2. Set the rip fence ¾ in. from the blade.

3. Fit a stop block to the rip fence so that the dado blade will cut 4⅞ in. into the top of the leg. This way the 5-in.-wide apron will cover the mortise.

4. Cut a stopped dado on one of the outside edges of each leg blank (see **photo F** on p. 132).

5. Reset the rip fence on the left side of the blade, again ¾ in. from the blade. Reposition the stock block on the other side of the fence as well. If your saw can't do this, set the fence 2⅛ in. from the blade.

6. Cut the second dado in the top of each leg.

7. Unplug your table saw.

8. Lay out the tenon template by holding a 2-in. by 4⅞-in. piece of ¼-in. plywood against the dado blade and sketching the curve of the blade on one end.

9. Cut the curve. The template should be a little bit smaller than the mortise so the tenon doesn't bottom out.

Cutting the tenons

1. Plug your table saw back in. Reset your dado blade to cut ³⁄₁₆ in. deep.

2. Mark the shoulders of the tenons the correct distance apart, centered on the

PHOTO E: Lay out the other three leg blanks from the completed first leg. This strategy allows you to change the design to accommodate mistakes or changes made in the first leg.

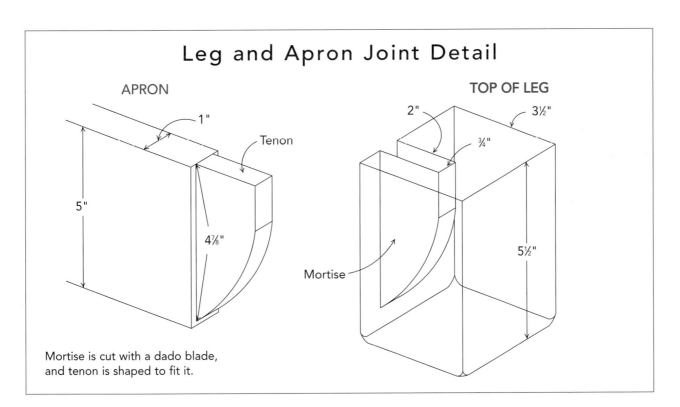

Leg and Apron Joint Detail

APRON

1"

Tenon

5"

4⅞"

Mortise is cut with a dado blade, and tenon is shaped to fit it.

TOP OF LEG

2"

3½"

¾"

Mortise

5½"

PHOTO F: Cut the mortises in the tops of the legs, using a table saw with a dado blade set at almost full height.

PHOTO G: Cut the apron tenon faces using a dado blade and miter gauge.

PHOTO H: Mark out the profile of the mortise on the tenon using a template.

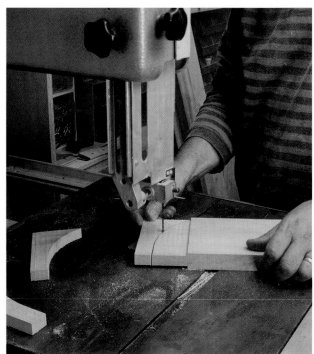

PHOTO I: Cut the tenon to size on a bandsaw. A jigsaw will work as well.

aprons (leaving at least 2 in. extra at each end). Set the rip fence as a stop.

3. Cut the tenons to thickness on all four aprons using the miter gauge to guide the workpieces (see **photo G**).

4. Align the tenon template on the tenon with the flat end flush with the top edge, and transfer the profile (see **photo H**).

5. Cut the tenon profiles on the bandsaw (see **photo I**).

Assembling the Base

1. Dry-fit the base, checking that the joints fit and that the top of the aprons and the legs are flush. Make any adjustments necessary.

2. Spread glue liberally in the mortises and on the tenons. Clamp the legs and aprons together (see **photo J**). If you don't have clamps long enough to reach across the full length of the base, you can double up the clamps. Let the glue set.

3. Mark center lines on the long aprons.

4. Cut the center support to length, then fit and clamp it between the long aprons.

5. To secure the center support, mark and drill two dowel holes through each long apron and into the center support.

6. Glue and hammer the dowels into the holes, leaving the heads proud.

7. Make a dowel template with two holes at the locations in the drawing on p. 127.

8. Place the tenon template over the tops of the each leg blank, and drill holes 2 in. deep (see **photo K** on p. 134). To secure each joint, the dowels need to go all the way through each tenon and into the other side of the mortise.

PHOTO J: Clamp up the base at one time, running clamps across each joint and the lengths of the sides. Double up clamps if you don't have any long enough.

PHOTO K: Using a template or other accurate layout, drill the holes for the dowel pins through the leg's mortise and tenon. The hole must be deep enough for the dowel to seat in the opposite mortise wall.

9. Glue and hammer the dowels into the holes, leaving the heads proud.

10. Clean up any glue squeeze-out from the dowels.

Attaching the top to the base

The top should be attached to the base with fasteners that allow for wood movement. The 36-in.-wide top can grow and shrink across its width quite a bit between the driest and wettest times of the year. I use commercial tabletop fasteners that are secured to the top but which slide in slots in the aprons.

1. Cut 21 biscuit slots in the apron at the locations indicated (see "Biscuit-Slot Locations" and **photo L**). You can use either a biscuit joiner or a router with a slot cutter to do this. How far down from the top edge of the aprons you cut depends on the particular type of tabletop fasteners you use. Set your biscuit joiner or router accordingly.

2. Lay the top upside down on the floor. Put a blanket down first, so you don't scratch the surface.

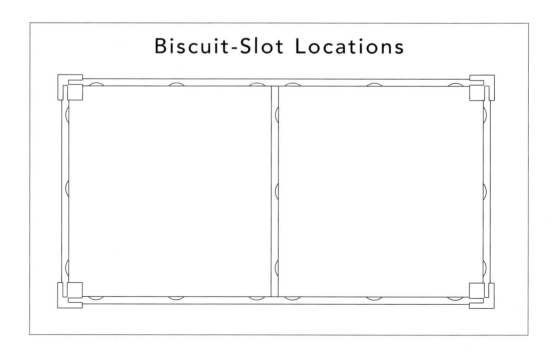

Biscuit-Slot Locations

PHOTO L: A biscuit joiner makes an excellent slot cutter for the tabletop fasteners.

3. Put the base upside down on the top, and center it.

4. Align the tabletop fasteners centered in their slots, and mark the screw holes in the top. Note that you need to locate the fasteners keeping in mind the direction the wood will move. If the wood is very wet, you can locate the fasteners tight against the long aprons; if the wood is dry, place them as far as possible from the aprons. The fasteners on the short aprons need only to be centered in their slots.

5. Drill pilot holes, then screw the fasteners in place (see **photo M**).

Waxing

The table gets a simple wax finish. Apply dark brown Briwax to the top, aprons, and legs. The dark wax lodges in and highlights any dents you've collected during construction, any scratches from skipping grits while sanding, and any other natural imperfections. The result looks believably 100 years old.

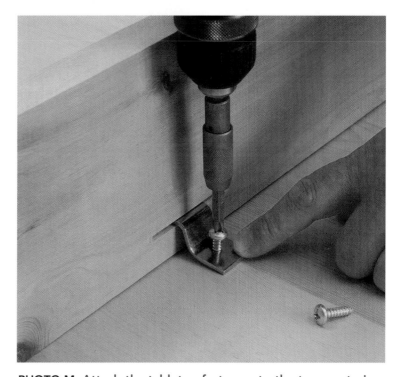

PHOTO M: Attach the tabletop fasteners to the top, centering them in the slots to allow for wood movement.

KITCHEN ISLAND AND STOOL

IN A LARGE KITCHEN, ESPECIALLY ONE with a U-shaped layout, an island can be a real time- and stepsaver. An island can anchor the room and organize the work flow, while providing accessible counter space from all directions.

There are no set guidelines for sizing an island, but there are a few rules for the spaces around it: For work aisles that face appliances, 42 in. is the suggested minimum, and there should be 36 in. between an island and wall. These standards help keep cooks from colliding and prevent appliance or cabinet doors on an island from banging into the ones opposite them when open.

This island is designed to separate the kitchen from another room. It has a storage side, which faces the kitchen, and on the opposite side is an overhang for stools. It could also work well as a traditional island by removing the overhang. Build-in one end and it will work as a peninsula.

This island is not presented as the best or most perfect island but something that is perhaps more difficult: an "average" island that is still appealing. It is an average size with average style. You can easily adapt the design to your kitchen. The details in this island, however, will show you what you need to know to construct your perfect island.

Also included are some easy-to-make handles and knobs. Sometimes these small details are just the thing to give your project that special zing.

Lastly, there's a sturdy, straightforward stool for those times when you want to sit and chat with the cook. A lot of people are hesitant to build seating, but as you can see by this example, a stool is really just an odd-looking table.

CENTER ISLAND

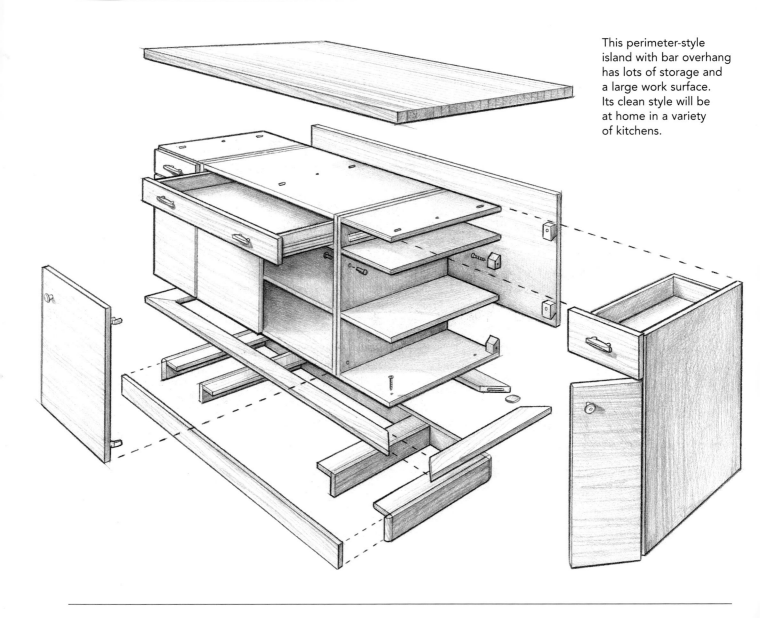

This perimeter-style island with bar overhang has lots of storage and a large work surface. Its clean style will be at home in a variety of kitchens.

Construction and Assembly

The island is constructed in sections or modules, which makes it manageable to build and easy to install. When I decided to make the doors plain (in an effort to allow the style to fit into as many existing kitchens as possible), I decided on flat doors, which might seem easy to make. The problem with flat doors is that unless they are perfectly flat they look terrible. No matter how much you adjust them, there are always one or two corners that stick out and interrupt the lines of the piece.

There are ways to make very flat doors, such as veneering over medium-density fiberboard (MDF) or honeycomb panels,

Views of Kitchen Island

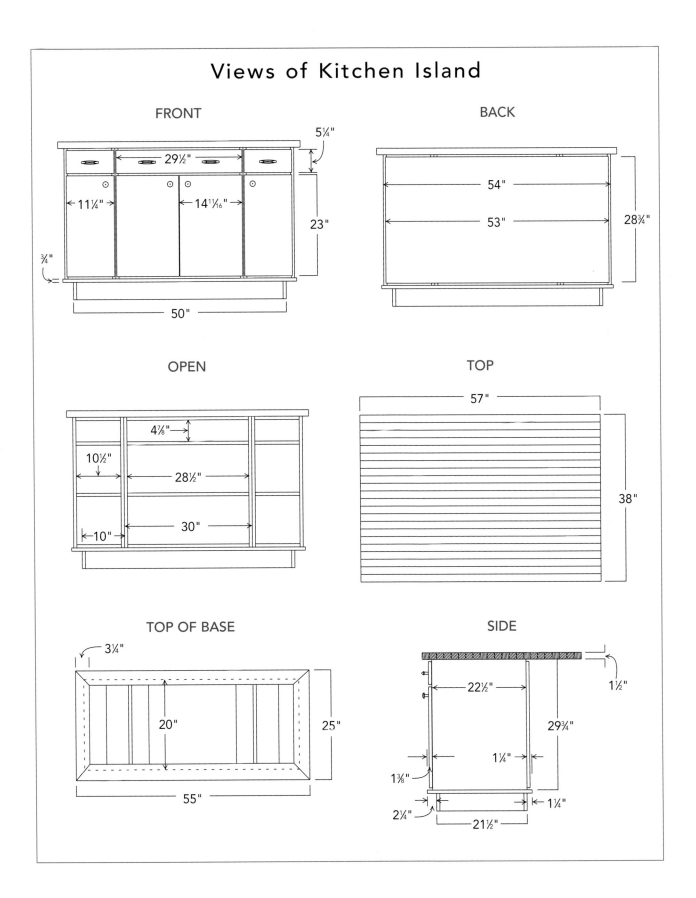

FRONT

BACK

OPEN

TOP

TOP OF BASE

SIDE

CUT LIST FOR CENTER ISLAND

Base

2	Pieces	4" x 48½" x ¾"	cherry plywood
8	Pieces	4" x 20" x ¾"	cherry plywood
4	Pieces	4" x 19⅞" x ¾"	cherry plywood
4	Pieces	4" x ¾" x ¾"	solid cherry

Base Frame

2	Pieces	55" x 3¼" x ¹¹⁄₁₆"	solid cherry
2	Pieces	25" x 3¼" x ¹¹⁄₁₆"	solid cherry

Cabinet Boxes

6	Sides	29¾" x 22½" x ¾"	cherry plywood
6	Tops, bottoms, dividers (outside boxes)	10½" x 22½" x ¾"	cherry plywood
3	Tops, bottoms, dividers (center box)	28½" x 22½" x ¾"	cherry plywood
2	Shelves (outside boxes)	10⁷⁄₁₆" x 22⅜" x ¾"	cherry plywood
1	Shelf (center box)	28⁷⁄₁₆" x 22⅜" x ¾"	cherry plywood

Back

1	Piece	53" x 28¾" x ¾"	cherry plywood

Fronts

2	Drawer fronts (outside drawers)	11¼" x 5¼" x ¾"	cherry plywood
1	Drawer front (center drawer)	29½" x 5¼" x ¾"	cherry plywood
2	Doors (outside)	11¼" x 23" x ¾"	cherry plywood
2	Doors (center)	14¹¹⁄₁₆" x 23" x ¾"	cherry plywood

Drawers

6	Sides	22" x 4" x ½" [12mm]	Baltic birch plywood
2	Fronts (outside drawers)	8½" x 4" x ½" [12mm]	Baltic birch plywood
1	Front (center drawer)	26½" x 4" x ½" [12mm]	Baltic birch plywood
2	Backs (outside drawers)	8½" x 4" x ½" [12mm]	Baltic birch plywood
1	Back (center drawer)	26½" x 4" x ½" [12mm]	Baltic birch plywood
2	Bottoms (outside drawers)	9" x 21¾" x ¼" [6mm]	Baltic birch plywood
1	Bottom (center drawer)	27" x 21¾" x ¼" [6mm]	Baltic birch plywood

Top

22	Pieces	1¾" x 1½" x 57"	solid maple

CUT LIST FOR CENTER ISLAND

Other materials

100 ft.	Edge tape	maple
4	Hinges	110° full overlay, European concealed
4	Hinges	110° half overlay, European concealed
3 pr.	Drawer glides	¾-extension, epoxy-coated, bottom-mount
12	Shelf-support pins	
8	Hex-drive connector bolts and threaded sleeves	
8	Confirmat screws	
	Mineral oil	
	Lacquer	

but I wanted to use plywood, which almost never stays perfectly flat. My solution was to create a design element that would disguise any twists that might occur: a ½-in. space between the doors and drawer fronts. To emphasize this detail, I used a contrasting wood for the edges of the doors and drawer fronts as well as for the cabinet.

Making the Base

Start by building the base. It is important that the base be solid. Clearly it has to support the weight of the entire island. More importantly, since an island needs to be fastened to the floor (so it doesn't move around), it has to be able to resist lifting forces applied when people push against the island and lean down on the overhang.

1. Rip two 4-in. by 48½-in. and eight 4-in. by 20-in. strips of cherry plywood.

2. Biscuit the 20-in.-long pieces into four units with an L-shaped profile. They should be biscuited along their 20-in. sides, so that the units are 4 in. high by 4¾ in. wide by 20 in. long when assembled.

3. Put these aside for now and cut four ¾-in. by ¾-in. by 4-in. pieces of solid cherry, and biscuit, glue, and clamp these onto the ends of the 48½-in. plywood pieces. These become the corners of the base and will pro-

tect the fragile plywood corners from being damaged by feet or vacuum cleaners.

4. Once the glue is dry, sand off any excess glue. Now you're ready to biscuit the frame together.

5. Align the long sides parallel and 20 in. apart.

6. Position the four L-shaped units between the sides (see **photo A** on p. 142). One L-shaped unit forms each end, and the remaining two are positioned with the 4-in. leg directly underneath where the individual boxes join together. Make sure the 4¾-in. legs face toward the center of the base. These four L-shaped units will not only support the cabinets but also provide a means of attaching them to the base.

7. Biscuit, glue, and clamp these parts together.

8. When the glue is dry, sand all surfaces flush and rout a ⅛-in. quarter-round on each solid corner. Then finish-sand the outside of the base to 150 grit.

Making and assembling the decorative base frame

The next step is the decorative mitered frame that separates the base from the cabinets.

1. Mill up four pieces of solid cherry, two at 3¼ in. by ¹¹⁄₁₆ in. by (a little over) 55 in. and

two 3¼ in. by ¹¹⁄₁₆ in. by (a little over) 25 in. The extra length is to give you some room creep-up on the cut when cutting the miters.

2. Carefully miter the corners so that you end up with a frame 55 in. by 25 in.

I used my miter gauge on my table saw to cut these miters, but a radial-arm saw or chopsaw would also work. The important thing is accuracy. There is no such thing as a miter joint that's "good enough." Either it's just right or it's a bad joint. A bad joint may open up down the road, even when using biscuits. When the frame moves seasonally, there could be a fair amount of stress on these joints from time to time.

3. Cut a slot for a #20 biscuit in each joint.

4. Biscuit, glue, and clamp the frame together.

5. When the frame is dry, sand all joints flush.

6. Rout a ⅛-in. quarter-round, top and bottom around the outside perimeter of the frame.

7. Cut four pieces of 3/4-in. plywood to 19⅞ in. long by 4¾ in. wide for spacers.

8. Screw the spacers on top of the L-shaped assemblies, centered, so they're ¹⁄₁₆ in. shy of the long base sides.

9. Position the base frame on top of the base, around the spacers (see **photo A**).

You are probably wondering why the frame is ¹¹⁄₁₆ in. thick and not ¾ in. Well, the frame basically sits loose on the base, held in position by the four pieces of ¾-in. plywood screwed to the top of the supports on the base. The ¾-in.-thick plywood, which is actually a little shy of ¾ in. thick, will be slightly higher than the frame and will take most of the weight of the cabinets.

Cabinet Boxes

1. Cut to size all the cherry plywood for the cabinet boxes. Use the dimensions in the cut list.

2. Cut biscuit slots for all the corner joints and the joints for the divider that separates the drawer section. These should be arranged so that the top, bottom, and divider (when joined) are between the sides.

3. This is also the time to cut the shelves. The shelves should be ¹⁄₁₆ in. smaller than the

DESIGN OPTION: TRAY STORAGE

The storage space in this island is pretty generic—just open drawers and cabinet space—but it doesn't have to remain that way. With a little extra thought and effort, you can customize the spaces for what you may need to store. There are many accessories you can buy, like pull-out storage baskets and drawer dividers, or you can make your own.

To get you started thinking along these lines, I have included an option my clients often ask me to include in their custom work.

Large trays or platters pose a difficult storage problem, but with just a couple of extra steps, you can include storage for these items in your island. You could also build this storage afterward or add it to an existing cabinet, by making it a separate box that slides into an existing space.

Before assembling one of the side cabinets, create some grooves in the top of the bottom of the cabinet and in the underside of the divider wide enough to fit some ¼-in. plywood panels. The spacing will depend on what exactly you wish to store, but you can always cut more grooves than you think you need and just use as many dividers as you want. The quickest way to cut these grooves is on your table saw using a dado blade.

Tray-Storage Option

This storage unit can be built as part of the cabinet (example B) or as a separate unit (example A) that can be built and inserted later. Spacing of the dividers is determined by the items that need to be stored.

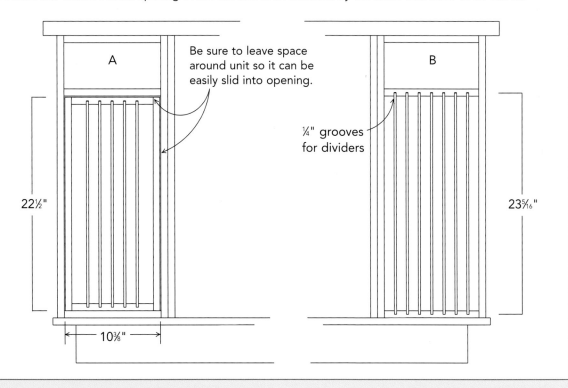

A

Be sure to leave space around unit so it can be easily slid into opening.

B

¼" grooves for dividers

22½"

23⁵⁄₁₆"

10⅜"

PHOTO B: Drill shelf pinholes for the adjustable shelves in the sides of the cabinets, using a commercial or shopmade jig.

width of the cabinet they fit into and ⅛ in. shorter front to back.

Shelf pinholes

The next step is to drill two rows of holes, front and back in each side within the middle 12 in. of the lower section of the cabinet for shelf pins to support the shelves (see **photo B**). The most common shelf pins fit into either 5mm or ¼-in. holes, so choose which you will use before you drill these holes.

A good formula for locating these holes is one-sixth the total width in from the front and back edges. I use a commercial jig made by Festo, but there are many jigs available; you can easily make your own by drilling a series of holes in a piece of plywood that fits the space. Even if the holes are not perfectly spaced, as long as each row is the same your shelves will lay flat. So make sure you always register the jig from the same edge.

Edgebanding

Before assembling the cabinet boxes, apply iron-on maple edgebanding to cover the exposed plywood edges. This includes all the front and back edges of the cabinets and the front edges of the shelves. The reason for banding the back edges of the cabinets is that, since the back is exposed and the back panel is recessed ½ in. all around, these edges will show. Iron-on edgebanding is available from many woodworking suppliers and is easy to apply.

1. Break off a piece a little longer than you need.

2. Apply the edging with an ordinary household iron, set on high temperature and no steam. Start at one end and move along the edge bit by bit, softening the glue as you go until the edging sticks.

3. Trim off the excess length by scoring it lightly on the glue side and snapping it off. The edging is slightly wider that the plywood, so sand it flush.

4. Continue to finish-sand all the insides of the cabinets, including both sides of the dividers and the shelves, to 150 grit.

5. Biscuit, glue, and clamp the boxes together and set them aside.

The back

1. Cut a piece of ¾-in. cherry plywood for the back panel and cover the edges with maple edgebanding.

Remember to account for the thickness of the edgebanding when you cut the back. The edgebanding adds approximately ³⁄₃₂ in. to the length and width of the panel so you must cut the back that much smaller before banding or you will have less than the ½-in. reveal that the design calls for. This is not all that critical for the back, but when you get to the doors and drawer fronts, it is very important.

2. Finish-sand the back.

3. While you are waiting for the glue on the cabinets to dry, you can make the angled blocks that attach the back panel to the cabinet boxes (see "Back-Panel Attachment Blocks").

BACK-PANEL ATTACHMENT BLOCKS

There are many ways to attach backs to cabinets, but few of them completely hide their joinery. Rabbets work well in solid wood, but in plywood cabinets, the edges would show. So I devised a very simple and easy knockdown method for this cabinet. This makes things simpler while building (giving access to the rear of cabinets for drawer-fitting and installation, for example) and is also more in line with its modular construction. In spite of being knockdown, it adds a lot of rigidity to the cabinet.

The back panel is attached using eight pairs of opposing-angled blocks. In the cabinets, one block is placed in each of the outside corners of the lower sections of the smaller boxes and in each of the four corners of the lower section of the center box. This arrangement allows the back to be lifted on and off easily. And the more you push down on it the tighter it wedges the back on. The location of the blocks in the corners keeps the cabinet boxes from racking.

The placement of the blocks is critical if the back is to be positioned correctly and be firmly attached. The blocks on the back panel itself must be as close as they can to where the sides of the cabinets will be without interfering with installing the back. All the blocks must be at exactly the right height, so that when the back is in place it is the correct height. So measure carefully. To make sure the back pulls tight to the cabinets before it bottoms out, position the blocks on the cabinets a little bit back from the edge (the thickness of the edge tape is a perfect distance).

The blocks are all identical: 2 in. long to the long point of the 45-degree bevel, 1½ in. wide, and ¾ in. thick. Screw the cabinet blocks to the side of the cabinets through their side, and screw the back-panel blocks to the panel through their face. After the cabinets are assembled with the back installed—and you are sure everything is right—remove the blocks, apply a little glue, and screw them back on.

Back-Panel Attachment Blocks

Keep blocks in lower part of cabinet or they will interfere with drawer.

Attachment blocks

Back panel

SIDE VIEW CUTAWAY

Cabinet side

Back panel

Attachment block

Screw

Attachment block

Position cabinet block back from the edge the thickness of the edge tape.

PHOTO C:
Assemble the
boxes separately,
then attach them
to the base and
to each other.

Cabinet Assembly

Connecting the boxes

At this point, you are ready to assemble
everything you have made so far.

1. Remove the clamps from the cabinet
boxes, and finish-sand the outsides.

2. Position the boxes on the base and temporarily clamp them together with all their
edges flush with their adjacent cabinets (see
photo C).

3. Mark out the holes for the connecting bolts.

I used two hex-drive connector bolts and
threaded sleeves along each of the front and
back edges. One 1¼ in. up and down from
the inside corners of the cabinets, all located
1¼ in. in from the outside edges. There are
several versions of this type of connector
available through woodworking suppliers,
and the one you choose will determine the
size of the hole you need to drill.

Connecting the
boxes to the base

1. Assuming the cabinets are still positioned
correctly on the base layout, drill holes

PHOTO D: Use hex-drive connector bolts and threaded
sleeves to connect the boxes to each other. Use Confirmat
screws to attach the boxes to the base.

through the bottom of the cabinets and into the crosspieces of the base (see **photo D**).
2. Screw the boxes down onto the base.

I used four Confirmat screws (also known as Euro screws) in the large center cabinet—one in each corner—and two each in the outside corners of the smaller cabinets. Again, the fasteners you choose will determine the size of the holes you drill. Make sure you position these holes far enough in that they clear the cherry frame on the top of the base.

Hanging the back
1. Make and attach the back-panel attachment blocks as described (see p. 145).
2. Hang the back in place and push down firmly (see **photo E**).

Drawer Construction and Installation

The drawers are constructed of ½-in. (12mm) Baltic birch plywood, biscuited together. You can certainly use solid wood if you prefer that look, but either way the construction is the same. The plywood boxes are slightly stronger because the orientation of the plies allows for more side-grain-to-side-grain gluing, in addition to the biscuits. The solid wood's end-grain-to-side-grain joint would rely primarily on the biscuits for strength. I have built both kinds of drawers, and I find either one works just fine in normal use.
1. Rip enough plywood 4 in. wide for the drawer boxes—sides, fronts, and backs.
2. Crosscut the pieces to length.
3. Pick out the back pieces of each drawer and rip them to 3⅜ in. wide. Making the backs of the drawers shallower will allow you to slide the drawer bottoms into the completed drawer boxes (see **photo F** on p. 148).
4. Leave the table saw set to 3⅜ in., and lower the blade to ¼ in. high.
5. Run a groove in the bottom inside edge of all the remaining parts.

PHOTO E: The back panel fits to the case with an attachment-block system.

6. Move the saw fence away from the blade by approximately half the width of the blade, and run the same parts through again. One more time, and you should have a groove wide enough for your ¼-in. drawer bottoms.

You could use a ¼-in.-wide dado blade, but by the time you got it set up, you could have the grooves cut with this method. You should have a piece of scrap handy as a test piece as well as a piece of the drawer-bottom material to test-fit the groove.
7. Size the groove so that the bottom fits snugly. If you have to reach for a hammer, the joint is too tight.
8. Sanding the drawer bottoms will remove enough material to allow you to slide them into the grooves easily.
9. Cut a slot for a #10 biscuit in each corner making sure that the front and back of the drawers fit between the sides.

PHOTO F: The drawers are made entirely from Baltic birch plywood and use biscuit joints at each corner.

10. Finish-sand the insides of all the parts, then biscuit, glue, and clamp the drawer boxes together.

11. When the glue is dry, finish-sand the outsides of the drawers.

12. Cut the bottoms to fit, finish-sand them, and slide them into their grooves. Fasten them in place with a couple of small screws along the back edge.

13. Mount the drawer glides and install the drawers in their openings (see "Size, Location, and Fit of Drawers").

I used standard European-style, ¾-extension undermount glides. As their name suggests, they mount to the bottom of the drawer box. I have installed enough of these kind of glides that I have a special jig for installing the cabinet side of the glides. There are, however, many different kinds and styles of drawer glides available, and your choice will determine the exact installation positioning and technique. This process is a lot easier with the back off.

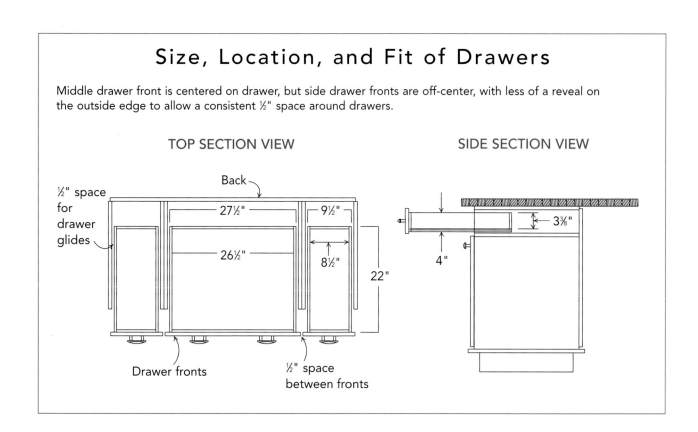

Size, Location, and Fit of Drawers

Middle drawer front is centered on drawer, but side drawer fronts are off-center, with less of a reveal on the outside edge to allow a consistent ½" space around drawers.

TOP SECTION VIEW

SIDE SECTION VIEW

½" space for drawer glides

Back

27½"

9½"

26½"

8½"

22"

Drawer fronts

½" space between fronts

3⅜"

4"

Hanging doors

Cut the cherry plywood for the doors and drawer fronts, and edge-band them as you did the cabinet parts. Remember to account for the thickness of the edgebanding, as you did with the back panel (see **photo G**).

1. Once you have these parts edged, finish-sand them to 150 grit and install the hinges.

I used 110-degree European concealed hinges. The specifics of installing these type of hinges is somewhat dependent on the brand of hinge you buy, so follow the manufacturer's instructions (see "Choosing Hinges").

2. Once you have this sorted out, hang the doors and adjust the hinges until you have

PHOTO G: Apply edgebanding to all the doors and drawer fronts. Sand the corners flush, when the glue sets.

CHOOSING HINGES

Be aware that you will have to use two different types of European hinges to hang the cabinet doors because of the ½-in. spacing between the doors and the ½-in. reveal around the edges. Let me explain.

The outside left and right doors overlay the cabinet side by ¼ in. (¾ in. less ½ in.) so you will need what is referred to as a half-overlay hinge. These hinges are designed to be used when two doors overlay a single ¾-in. cabinet side. They would normally position the door ⁵⁄₁₆ in. over the edge of the cabinet side, but ¼ in. is still within their adjustment range.

The center cabinet doors overlay their cabinet sides by ½ in. because there are two sides fastened together here, which adds up to 1½ in. Subtract the ½-in. space between the doors and you have 1 in. or ½-in. overlay per door. For these doors, you will need what is referred to as a full-overlay hinge. These are normally used when one door covers a ¾-in. cabinet side. They normally position a door a little over ⅝ in. over the edge of the cabinet side, but ½ in. is within their adjustment range.

½ in. at the outside edges and ½ in. between and under the doors (see **photo H**).

Attaching drawer fronts

The drawer fronts are easier than the doors, but you will need a helper.

1. Cut some ½-in. spacer blocks from scrap wood, and place them on top of the doors.

2. Position the drawer fronts one at a time on the spacers and align them side to side with the door or doors under them.

3. Place the palm of one hand on the back of the drawer box (the back panel is still off, right?) and the palm of your other hand on the drawer front and squeeze tightly as you open the drawer. This holds the drawer front in place while your helper places a couple of spring clamps on the drawer to hold the front in place.

4. From the inside of the drawer, drill four holes for the screws that attach the drawer front to the drawer box. Locate these holes 1¼ in. from the sides and 1¼ in. from the top and bottom of the drawer (see **photo I**). A small block 1¼ in. square will help you locate where to drill these holes.

If you find that you still need some adjustment, remove the front and enlarge the hole in the drawer box. This will give you a little room to move the drawer front around. There are special screws available for this application with extra large heads, but a screw and a washer works just as well.

PHOTO H: Hang the doors using 110° concealed hinges. They should hang flush with the fronts of the cabinet boxes.

PHOTO I: Attach the drawer fronts to the drawer boxes, using spring clamps to hold them in place as you drill and then screw them together.

Making the Butcher-Block Top

Making your own butcher-block top, while not difficult, is a lot of work and takes a lot of time. There is something to be said for buying a commercially made top. If this was a normal width counter top (24 in.), I would probably have done just that, since they are relatively inexpensive. Unfortunately, this top is 38 in. wide; if you could find one this wide, it would be much more expensive.

The first thing to consider in a solid-wood top is stability. You want the top to be flat, straight, square, and rigid and to remain that way. The best way to accomplish this is to use quartersawn wood, but since slabs of quartersawn wood large enough to produce this top are rare, a butcher-block top is a better option.

The top of this island is 1½ in. thick, which is a little thicker than an average countertop. Any thinner, though, and it just doesn't look substantial enough. You could make it thicker, but then you would have to build the base lower since your island would be higher than the standard 36 in.

1. Rip 8/4 flatsawn stock into 22 strips approximately 1⅝ in. wide and a little longer than the top.

2. Joint and thickness-plane the strips to 1¾ in. by 1½ in.

3. Glue the strips together in groups of five and six, then glue the groups together (see **photo J**). This will produce a quartersawn top 38½ in. wide, 1½ in. thick, and a little longer than 57 in. The extra width and length is for trimming the top straight and square later.

PHOTO J: Glue up the butcher-block top, first in groups of five and six pieces. Then after the glue sets, glue the assemblies together.

PHOTO K: Trim the ends of the top square with the edges. I used a circular saw and guide for this work.

If these strips are really straight and square you should have no trouble gluing up the top without biscuits, dowels, or splines. But if your stock is a little wild, don't hesitate to use them. Don't try to glue this top together all at once. It is difficult to spread glue quickly over so many surfaces and then get them aligned and evenly clamped. You will almost certainly lose control over some of them at some point and end up with a less-than-perfect top.

4. Sand the top flat when completely glued up and dry.

I used a stationary drum sander. If you don't have such a machine, you can thickness the smaller groups with a planer as you glue them up and then flatten the completed top with a handplane. Alternatively, you can have the finished top thickness-sanded at a commercial shop.

5. Rip the top to width and trim the ends. I used a straightedge/saw combination designed for this kind of operation, but a router and a straightedge would work fine (see **photo K**).

Finishing

I finished the island with satin spray lacquer and used a polymerized tung oil for the top. You can also use mineral oil for the top, but it won't wear as well and, once cured, the tung oil is safe for food surfaces, which is the main reason for using mineral oil. It really depends on what you plan to use your island for.

Attaching the Island to the Floor and the Top to the Island

Once you have the island completed, you will want to put it into use. There is more to this, however, than just setting it into place and laying on the top. Once in position, your island should be leveled, then firmly attached to the floor. This is more easily accomplished if you first remove the cabinet boxes from the base. Then you can shim and/or scribe the base level and attach it to the floor with some angle irons from the inside of the base. (This hardware is available from any hardware store or building center.) With the base secured to the floor, you can reassemble the cabinet boxes on the base and attach the top.

To attach the top, create eight elongated holes or slots in the tops of the cabinets: one in each corner of the center cabinet and two in the outside corners of each side cabinet. These slots should run front to back and will allow for seasonal wood movement without damaging either the cabinets or the top. Then attach the top through these holes with screws and washers.

Handles and Knobs

Decorative hardware is easily made and will set your project apart.

HANDLE

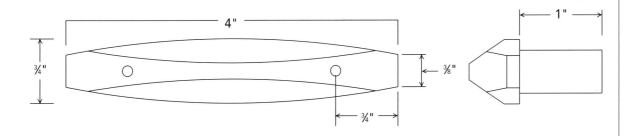

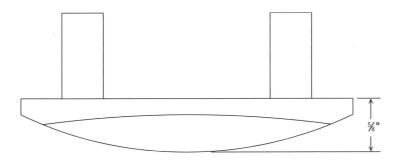

KNOB

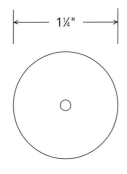

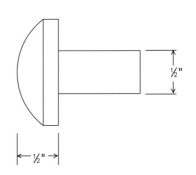

Steps for Shaping Handles

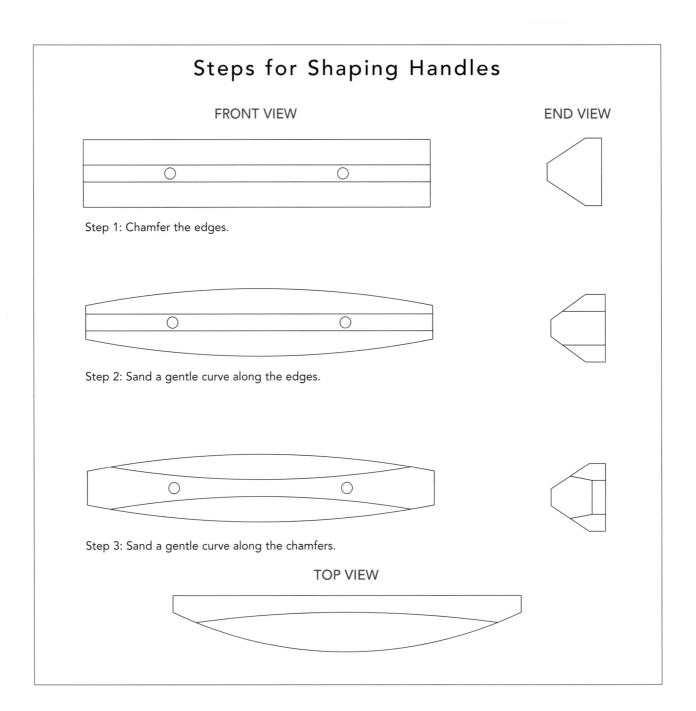

FRONT VIEW

END VIEW

Step 1: Chamfer the edges.

Step 2: Sand a gentle curve along the edges.

Step 3: Sand a gentle curve along the chamfers.

TOP VIEW

CUT LIST FOR HANDLES AND KNOBS

4	Handles	¾" x ⅝" x 4"	bird's-eye maple
4	Knobs	1½" x 1½" x ½"	bird's-eye maple

Other materials

1	Dowel	½" dia.	maple
10	Trim-head screws (black)	1⅝"	

Making the Handles

These handles have graceful curves but need no special jigs or techniques to create. They're so small, they can simply be sanded into shape (see "Steps for Shaping Handles").

1. Mill a piece of bird's-eye maple ¾ in. by ⅝ in. and long enough to make the handles you need plus a couple extra (just in case).

2. Rip a 30-degree angle along both ⅝-in.-wide edges, leaving a ³⁄₁₆-in. flat on each edge (see **photo L**).

3. Crosscut the piece into 4-in. lengths.

4. Belt-sand curves on each of the edges you just beveled. Create a curve that goes from nothing in the center, flowing down to ³⁄₁₆ in. on each end (see **photo M**).

5. Sand a curve on the face of each piece that goes from nothing in the center curving down to ⁷⁄₁₆ in. on each end (see **photo N**). Make sure that you use a belt with the finest grit you have. You don't want to have to do a lot of finish-sanding that might soften the angles and planes you have created—you want them to remain crisp.

PHOTO L: Carefully rip a 30° angle on the edges of the blanks for the handles.

PHOTO M: Sand the top and bottom curves on the handle blanks. A stationary sander, or a belt sander in a vise, works well for this.

PHOTO N: Sand the curve on the face of the handles in the same way.

PHOTO O: Turn the faces of the knobs on a lathe, using whatever turning tool you're most comfortable with.

PHOTO P: Attach the handles and knobs to the doors and drawer fronts with mounting studs and screws.

Making the Knobs

The knobs are turned on a lathe.

1. Screw a piece of scrap plywood to a small faceplate. Attach a square of bird's-eye maple approximately 1½ in. square and ½ in. thick to the plywood, using some double-sided tape.

2. Mount this assembly on the lathe. Using a parting tool, create a 1¼-in.-dia. circle.

3. Using a small gouge or a skew chisel, whichever you find more comfortable, shape the face into a dome leaving ³⁄₁₆ in. of flat around the outside edge (see **photo O**).

4. While it's still on the lathe, sand the knob to 150 grit.

5. Make the other three knobs.

6. On your drill press, drill holes for the trim-head screws in the center of each knob. Also, drill holes for the handles ¾ in. in from each end of the handles, centered top to bottom.

7. Cut a ½-in.-dia. maple dowel into ⅝-in. lengths for the mounting studs, and drill a pilot hole through the center of each. This hole will accept the screws that attach the handles and knobs to the drawers and doors. A good way to hold these small parts for drilling is to clamp them in a handscrew.

8. Attach the handles and knobs to the doors and drawers with trim-head screws through these mounting studs (see **photo P**).

Finishing

I finished these parts with the same oil I used on the top of the island, but any furniture oil will do. Oil brings out the figure a little better than a lot of spray finishes and will allow the handles and knobs to acquire a nice patina over time from handling.

STURDY, STRAIGHTFORWARD STOOL

This ash stool uses a combination of biscuit joinery and dowels for solid, effective construction.

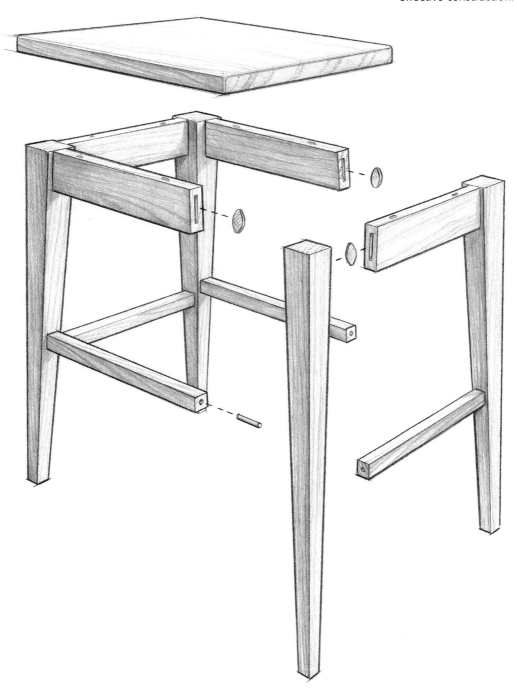

Views of Stool

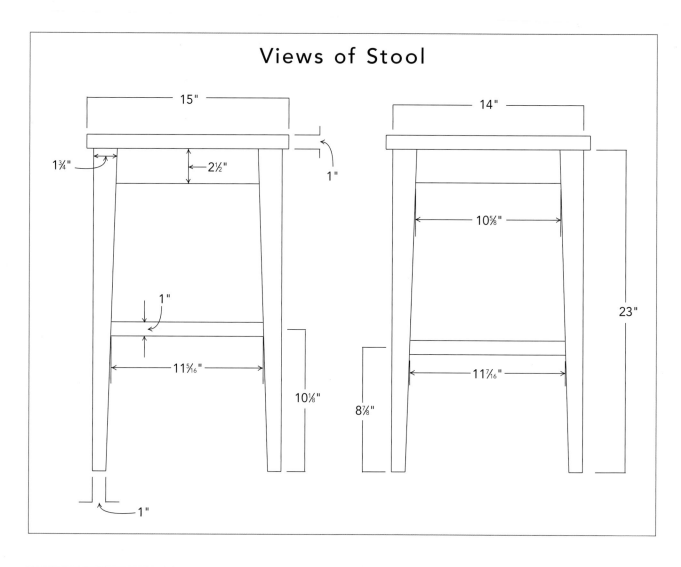

CUT LIST FOR STOOL

1	Seat	15" x 15" x 1"	ash
4	Legs	1¾" x 1¾" x 23"	ash
4	Aprons	2½" x 10⅝" x 1"	ash
4	Stretchers	1" x 1" x 12⁹⁄₁₆"	ash

Milling the Parts

This piece is constructed entirely of solid wood, so since you have a fair amount of milling to do, it's a good idea to do it all at once.

1. Mill all the parts for the legs, aprons, and stretchers to the dimensions in the cut list.

Leave all but the legs a little longer than finished size.

2. Mill at least three pieces to glue up for the seat. I prefer to use an odd number of boards when I do solid-wood glue-ups and to alternate the growth rings in adjacent boards. This way any cupping should average out rather than having the entire piece cup in one direction.

Tapering the Legs

The legs taper on the two inside faces from 1¾ in. at the top (the full thickness of the leg) to 1 in. at the bottom.

1. Make a simple jig made of plywood with two stops angled to register the leg in the cut (see "Leg Tapering Jig").

PHOTO Q: Taper the legs for the stool using a table-saw jig.

2. Place the leg in the jig with your table-saw fence set to the width of the jig's plywood base. Run it through your saw (see **photo Q**).
3. Rotate the leg 90 degrees, and run it through again.
4. Repeat the process for all the legs.

Sizing and Joinery for the Aprons and Stretchers

The apron and stretcher pieces meet the legs on the tapered sides so they will have to be crosscut at the same angle.
1. Lay one apron piece and one stretcher under two legs with the top of the apron piece flush with the tops of the legs and the stretcher placed the correct distance up from the bottom of the legs. Make sure the legs are parallel to each other and square to the apron and stretcher.
2. Mark where the legs cross the apron and stretcher. Remember that there are two different stretcher locations, so you will have to do this twice (see **photo R** on p. 160).

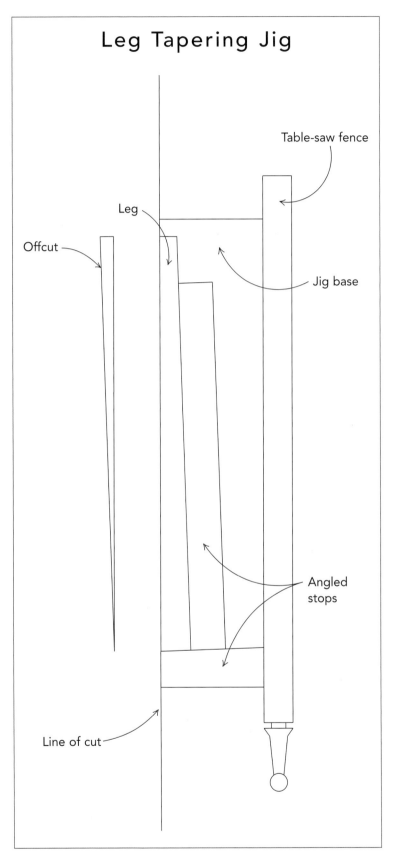

Leg Tapering Jig

Table-saw fence

Leg

Offcut

Jig base

Angled stops

Line of cut

PHOTO R: Mark the angles and intersections of the legs, aprons, and stretchers using the actual parts, not measurements.

PHOTO S: Single biscuits join the tops of the legs to the aprons.

3. Crosscut these parts to length at the marked angle on your table saw using your miter gauge.

4. Drill countersunk holes in the underside of the apron pieces large enough to easily accept the heads of the screws and deep enough to allow the screws to enter the seat approximately ¾ in. The seat will be attached to the base with two screws through each of the apron pieces.

5. Drill oversized holes the rest of the way through the pieces. The oversized holes will allow the seat to expand and contract seasonally without damaging either the seat or the base.

6. Cut the biscuit slots that connect the apron pieces to the legs (see **photo S**). The apron pieces are recessed ½ in. from the outside faces of the legs so you will have to set your biscuit-joiner fence deeper when you cut the slots in the legs; otherwise, these are

PHOTO T: Drill holes for dowels in the ends of the stretchers and in the sides of the legs. I used a horizontal borer for this work.

normal #20 biscuit joints. Making the recess exactly ½ in. is not critical—a little more or less is fine.

7. Drill ⅜-in.-dia. holes in the center of the ends of the stretchers and centered on the legs at the correct heights (remember there are two different heights). I used a horizontal-mortising machine, but a drill press with a little care, ingenuity, and a jig will work fine—just mind how the tapers pull the drill bit to one side (see **photo T**).

Assembly

Assembly is pretty straightforward: The biscuit joints and the dowel joints get glued and clamped together. To make your life easier, however, I suggest that you assemble the stool in stages.

1. Before starting assembly, finish-sand all the parts to 150 grit. This is also a good time

PHOTO U: Assemble the stool frame in stages: First glue up two sets of legs, aprons, and stretchers; then attach the two assemblies with the remaining aprons and stretchers.

to size and finish-sand the seat (I'm sure it's dry by now).

2. Glue and clamp two sets of legs, an apron, and a stretcher, and set them aside to dry.

3. When dry, you can easily connect these two assemblies with the remaining apron pieces and stretchers (see **photo U** on p. 161).

Finishing

I finished the stool with a satin spray lacquer, but a nice oil finish would also look nice and feel better to the touch. When you are done with the finishing, attach the seat (see **photo V**).

PHOTO V: Screw the stool frame to the seat through the aprons.

DESIGN OPTION: UPHOLSTERED SEAT

I think this is a nice-looking stool as is. But if you want to dress it up a little and make it more comfortable, it is a simple matter to replace the seat with an upholstered version.

In one way, this is actually easier to make since you don't have to construct the solid-wood seat. A piece of plywood makes an excellent base for the upholstery and has the benefit of being dimensionally stable so you don't have to take seasonal movement into account.

An upholstered seat is more comfortable and not that difficult to make.

You will need to purchase an 18-in. square of fabric and a 16-in. square of 2-in. high-density foam for each seat. Most fabric stores will carry both items.

1. Cut a piece of ¾-in. plywood 14 in. by 14 in. When centered on the base, this will leave ½ in. all around that will be taken up with foam.

2. Take the square of foam and bevel the outside edge so that the square is 14 in. by 14 in. on the bottom and 16 in. by 16 in. on the top. A bandsaw works surprisingly well for this, but a sharp handsaw or bread knife will also work (the result doesn't have to be pretty).

3. Using some spray contact cement, glue this foam to the plywood.

4. Place this assembly upside-down on the fabric.

5. Fold and stretch one side of the fabric up and across the plywood until the foam folds up and covers the edge of the plywood. Staple it in place.

6. Repeat this on all four sides. At this point, you will have a fabric pocket at each corner. Pull and stretch these pockets diagonally across the plywood, and staple in place.

That's it! If this was your first time doing this, there is a good chance it doesn't look all that great. Don't despair—just remove the staples and try again. It's a matter of getting the stretching right and sometimes it takes a few tries.

Cross Section of Upholstered Seat

A sandwich of plywood, foam, and fabric makes an attractive and comfortable seat.

Fabric

2" foam

14" square of ¾" plywood

Finished seat

Fabric is folded under plywood, compressing foam to 1" and pulling beveled edge down to fill ½" space around the edge of the plywood, for a finished 15"-square seat.

Staple fabric to plywood.

METRIC CONVERSION CHART

Inches	Centimeters	Millimeters	Inches	Centimeters	Millimeters
⅛	0.3	3	13	33.0	330
¼	0.6	6	14	35.6	356
⅜	1.0	10	15	38.1	381
½	1.3	13	16	40.6	406
⅝	1.6	16	17	43.2	432
¾	1.9	19	18	45.7	457
⅞	2.2	22	19	48.3	483
1	2.5	25	20	50.8	508
1¼	3.2	32	21	53.3	533
1½	3.8	38	22	55.9	559
1¾	4.4	44	23	58.4	584
2	5.1	51	24	61.0	610
2½	6.4	64	25	63.5	635
3	7.6	76	26	66.0	660
3½	8.9	89	27	68.6	686
4	10.2	102	28	71.1	711
4½	11.4	114	29	73.7	737
5	12.7	127	30	76.2	762
6	15.2	152	31	78.7	787
7	17.8	178	32	81.3	813
8	20.3	203	33	83.8	838
9	22.9	229	34	86.4	864
10	25.4	254	35	88.9	889
11	27.9	279	36	91.4	914
12	30.5	305			

RESOURCES

ADAMS WOOD PRODUCTS
P.O. Box 728
Morristown, TN 37815-0728
(423) 587-2942
*Premade table and furniture legs
and feet*

GARRETT WADE
161 Avenue of the Americas
New York, NY 10013
(800) 221-2942
*Polymerized tung oil, epoxy, specialty
woodworking tools and supplies*

HARTVILLE TOOL CO.
13163 Market Ave. N.
Hartville, OH 44632
(800) 345-2396
*BriWax, turntables, European concealed
hinges, tools, and woodworking supplies*

HIGHLAND HARDWARE
1045 N. Highland Ave. NE
Atlanta, GA 30306
(800) 241-6748
*Finishing supplies, tools, and wood-
working supplies*

MBK ENTERPRISES, INC.
P.O. Box 7692
Hilton Head Island, SC 29938
(843) 342-3003
Ellipse Master (ellipse and circle jig)

McFEELY'S
1620 Wythe Rd.
Lynchburg, VA 24501
(800) 443-7937
*Screws, fasteners, threaded inserts,
hanger bolts, tools, and woodworking
supplies*

**ROCKLER WOODWORKING
AND HARDWARE**
4365 Willow Dr.
Medina, MN 55340
(800) 279-4441
*Drawer glides, shelf-support pins, hard-
ware, tools, and woodworking supplies*

SELECT MACHINERY, INC.
6430 Ellwell Crescent
Rego Park, NY 11374
(718) 897-3937
*Lamello biscuit joiners, biscuits,
and accessories*

TOOLGUIDE CORP.
1187 Coast Village Rd., Suite 1215
Santa Barbara, CA 93108
(888) 463-3786
*Festo (FS-LR 32mm hole-drilling system
and other Festo power tools)*

WOODCRAFT
P.O. Box 1686
560 Airport Industrial Rd.
Parkersburg, WV 26102
(800) 225-1153
*Specialty woods, Watco Danish Oil, con-
nector bolts, tabletop fasteners, keyhole
hangers, hardware, tools, and woodworking supplies*

WOODWORKER'S SUPPLY
1108 North Glen Rd.
Casper, WY 82601
(800) 645-9292
*Veneer edge tape, circle cutters, rubber
bumpers, hardwood dowels, dowel pins,
hardware, tools, and woodworking
supplies*

INDEX

INDEX